Aucuba japonica variegata

AN ILLUSTRATED GUIDE TO

FOLIAGE

HOUSEPLANTS

Brighten your home throughout the year with this stunning selection of easy-care plants

Pilea cadierei nana

Cryptanthus bromelioides 'It'

AN ILLUSTRATED GUIDE TO
FOLIAGE
HOUSEPLANTS

Brighten your home throughout the year with this stunning selection of easy-care plants

William Davidson

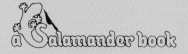

a Salamander book

Published by Arco Publishing, Inc.
NEW YORK

A Salamander Book

Published by Arco Publishing Inc.,
215 Park Avenue South,
New York, N.Y. 10003,
United States of America

© Salamander Books Ltd., 1982
Salamander House,
27 Old Gloucester Street,
London WC1N 3AF,
United Kingdom.

ISBN 0 668 06196 0

Library of Congress Catalog Card
No. 83-83422

All correspondence concerning the
content of this book should be addressed
to Salamander Books Ltd.

Contents

Text and colour photographs are cross-
referenced throughout as follows: 64◗

The plants are arranged in alphabetical
order of Latin name. Page numbers in
bold refer to text entries; those in *italics*
refer to photographs.

Credits

Author: William Davidson is involved with all aspects of houseplants, and has been employed by Rochfords, Europe's leading growers, for most of his working life. His interests encompass growing, exhibiting, writing, consultancy, lecturing, as well as radio and television programmes. He is the author of many successful books on houseplants.

Editor: Geoffrey Rogers
Designer: Roger Hyde

Photographs: All the photographs in the book have been taken by Eric Crichton. © Salamander Books Ltd.
Line drawings: Tyler/Camoccio Design Consultants. © Salamander Books Ltd.
Colour reproductions: Rodney Howe Ltd., England.
Monochrome: Bantam Litho Ltd., England
Filmset: SX Composing Ltd., England.

Printed in Belgium by
Henri Proost & Cie, Turnhout.

Introduction

Over the past three decades, houseplants in all shapes and sizes have shown an astonishing increase in popularity. The previous most popular time for indoor plants was at the turn of the century, when many foliage and flowering plants were brought in from tropical regions. Most were kept in heated glasshouses and conservatories, to be removed and put to use as indoor subjects for limited periods, as few homes were warm enough or light enough to sustain plants for more than a limited period. However, some – such as palms, ferns and the indestructible aspidistra – were able to cope with the spartan conditions.

Central heating, better light and generally more agreeable modern living conditions have done much to popularize houseplants, and an incredible range of decorative plants is now well within the scope of the more adventurous grower.

Selection

There are all sorts of aids that one can use in order to improve plants' well-being; but getting the right plants at the beginning can often prove to be the best approach. It is essential that plants for sale are stored in heated premises which are reasonably light and able to offer plants agreeable conditions while they are awaiting a purchaser; low temperatures can soon prove fatal to delicate plants. When selecting, look for plants that are fresh and free of blemishes. It may also help if the plant has a care card with some directions on plant care attached.

Early care

Any plant purchased during the winter should be carefully wrapped by the retailer and protected from cold on the way home. Place the plant inside a heated car if the journey home is of any length, and at all costs avoid putting tender plants in the unheated boot of a car.

Winter-purchased plants will be the most difficult to establish indoors and should be carefully unwrapped, watered if necessary, and placed in a temperature of around 18°C (65°F) in reasonable light to give them the best possible chance of adjusting to an entirely new set of conditions. Almost all plants will have been grown in heated greenhouses and will take unkindly to a sudden lowering of temperature.

Winter feeding should not be necessary, but plants bought at other times should be fed soon after they are brought indoors, and feeding should continue on a regular basis while they are in active growth. Plants bought in summer that are obviously too large for their growing pots can to advantage be potted into slightly larger containers without too much delay.

Temperature and location

One should check the care tag that comes with the plant and endeavour to match as nearly as possible the recommended temperature. Some plants need cooler conditions than others, and only a few of those that are generally available will need a very high temperature that exceeds 21°C (70°F). Avoid cold conditions and draughts, as these conditions can have very ill effects.

Brightly coloured and variegated plants will generally require to be grown in lighter conditions than those that have entirely green foliage, such as *Rhoicissus rhomboidea*. For poor light locations select green-foliaged subjects. Avoid placing plants in the hot stream of air ascending from heating appliances, and keep them out of very strong, direct sunlight.

Watering and feeding
Just about the most important requirement of all potted plants indoors is correct watering. Some, such as philodendrons, need moist soil, but most will be better for a good watering and a period of reasonable drying out before further water is given. Tepid water will be more suitable than cold water, and rain water will suit some plants better than hard tap water. Less water is generally needed in winter, and a combination of cold and wetness can be particularly damaging for many plants.

Never overfeed, and never feed plants that are ailing or have been freshly potted. Winter feeding is seldom necesary, and when feeding while plants are growing one should ensure that the directions on the fertilizer being used are followed, bearing in mind that too much may be more harmful than too little.

Potting
The fine root system of most potted plants will require an open and peaty potting mixture which they can easily penetrate and grow into, so garden soil is seldom suitable. Use a properly prepared mixture that contains a lot of peat and incorporates a balanced fertilizer that will sustain the plant. The new pot should be only a little larger than the old one. Following potting, the soil should be well watered, then watered sparingly, so that roots will seek moisture and establish more readily in the new container.

Grouping
Large and stately plants make an impressive feature in a room, but it will often be found that smaller plants have much more appeal if they are placed in small groups. Plants in groups create their own humidity and will grow better, especially in a dry atmosphere.

Propagation
Plants with large leaves are difficult to propagate indoors, but there is a wide range of subjects with smaller leaves, which will be reasonably easy to manage. Clean peat should be used, and a small heated propagation will be an asset, as will a rooting powder or liquid. Temperatures in the region of 21°C (70°F) and a close atmosphere will encourage cuttings to root more rapidly. Provide reasonable light for cuttings, but avoid direct sunlight.

Ailing plants
Sick plants should be carefully nursed back to good health, and this will mean no feeding, a minimal amount of water, and keeping plants in warm conditions but out of direct sunlight. There should be no attempt to disturb plant roots, or to pot it into fresh soil.

Above: **Acorus gramineus**
An easy-care, grassy-foliaged plant that does well in low temperatures if kept moist and in reasonable light. 17♦

Right: **Abutilon sevitzia**
A colourful, free-growing plant that thrives in moderate temperatures. Prune to shape at any time. 17♦

Below right:
Aglaonema 'Silver Queen'
A member of the Araceae family, this plant thrives in warm conditions. 18♦

Below: **Adiantum**
These come in many varieties, mostly with delicate foliage that is a perfect foil for other plants. 18♦

Above:
Aglaonema pseudobracteatum
*An interesting subject for adding
height and colour to collections.* 19◆

Below: **Alocasia indica**
*For the skilled plant person; needs
high humidity and constant warmth.
Veined leaves are a big plus.* 19◆

Above: **Alpinia sanderae**
Narrow, green-and-white variegated leaves are carried on tall, slender stems. Careful cultivation is necessary to retain colouring and to prevent loss of leaves. 20♦

11

Above: **Aralia elegantissima**
A striking plant with very dark green, almost black, foliage that is delicate on young plants but becomes coarse with age. Needs warmth. 21♦

Left: **Ananas bracteatus striatus**
An extremely ornamental member of the bromeliad family that will develop dazzling colour in good light. 20♦

Right: **Anthurium crystallinum**
The large, boldly veined leaves of this plant are impressive and best supported. A subject for very warm, humid conditions. 21♦

13

Left: **Aralia sieboldii variegata**
A truly splendid plant with broad, palmate leaves radiating from a stout central stem. Splendidly coloured in pale green and cream. 22♦

Below left: **Araucaria excelsa**
Composed of a multitude of fresh green, pine-needle leaves attached to tiered layers of spreading stems that themselves are arranged on a stout central stem. 22♦

Right: **Ardisia crispa (crenulata)**
Firm, shrubby plants with oval-shaped leaves of very dark green colouring that are waved along their margins. Because of their slow rate of growth, these are excellent where space is limited. 23♦

Below: **Asparagus meyerii**
A distinctive plant, producing long, cylindrical pale green growths. Growth emanates from soil level in the centre of the pot and sprays out in all directions. 24♦

Above: **Asplenium nidus avis**
*Smooth, pale green leaves radiate
from the centre in an attractive
arrangement. Needs moist
conditions.* 25♦

Below:
Aucuba japonica variegata
*The spotted laurel has pleasingly
variegated foliage and is a very tough
plant for cooler conditions.* 26♦

Abutilon sevitzia
- Good light
- Temp: 13-18°C (55-65°F)
- Frequent feeding

Vigorous growing plant for cooler conditions that offer good light, but not full sun when close to glass. Has attractively variegated maple-type leaves and pendulous orange-coloured flowers not unlike a small single hollyhock.

A loam-based mixture is essential when potting plants on – a task that must not be neglected if plants are to do as well as they can. While in active growth feed at every watering, to keep colour. Firm cuttings about 10cm (4in) in length will root readily in peaty mixture if placed in a heated propagator; when growth begins, remove the growing tip of the cutting. When well cared for, individual stems will put on 90cm (3ft) of growth in one season, but pruning can be undertaken at any time to limit growth. Never allow plants to stand in water for long periods, but water copiously while fresh leaves appear.

Soft growth attracts many pests, so a careful and frequent check is advised, especially under the leaves.

Take care
Whitefly can be a nuisance. 9♦

Acorus gramineus variegata
(Sweet flag)
- Grows anywhere
- Temp: 7-13°C (45-55°F)
- Keep moist

Not particularly attractive as an individual, but a fine plant for grouping with others. Well suited for inclusion in a bottle garden or converted fishtank, the acorus has a distinctive shape and is not invasive. Grassy foliage is green and gold in colour and produces neat clumps that may be divided at almost any time in order to produce new plants.

Very much the average indoor plant, it will respond well to a modicum of attention, but abhors hot and dry conditions and too much fussing over. A light location with protection from strong sun is best, and it will not object to some fresh air from open windows on warmer days.

Few pests seem to bother this plant, but in hot and dry conditions red spider may make an appearance and should be treated with one of the many available insecticides as soon as detected. When potting on, a loam-based mixture is best, but one should avoid putting plants into very large pots.

Take care
Divide every second year. 8♦

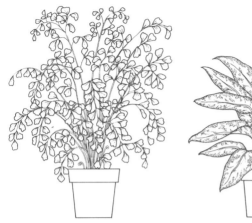

Adiantum
(Maidenhair fern)
- Light shade
- Temp: 18-21°C (65-70°F)
- Moist surroundings

Numerous varieties are available of these most delicate and beautiful foliage plants, whose pale green foliage contrasts with their black stems.

Bright, direct sunlight and dry atmospheric conditions will prove fatal. Offer maidenhair ferns lightly shaded positions in a warm room: place plants in a larger container and surround their pots with a moisture-retaining material such as peat. Misting of foliage is often recommended, but this exercise can have undesirable effects if the surrounding air temperature is inadequate. It is therefore better to use the mister to wet the soil surface.

Avoid use of chemicals on foliage. When potting on, a peaty mixture is needed, and once plants have established in their pots weak liquid feeding will be needed every time the plant is watered. During winter, feeding is not important and watering should be only sufficient to keep the soil moist.

Take care
Slugs find this foliage desirable. 8♦

Aglaonema crispum 'Silver Queen'
(Silver spear)
- Light shade
- Temp:18-21°C (65-70°F)
- Keep moist

There are numerous aglaonemas that form central clumps that increase in size as plants mature, but the variety A. 'Silver Queen' is superior in all respects. Individual spear-shaped leaves are produced at soil level and have a grey-green background colouring liberally spotted with silver.

New plants are made by separating the clumps at any time of year and potting them individually in a peaty mixture in small pots. As plants mature they can be potted on into slightly larger containers, and will in time produce offsets of their own. For the second and subsequent potting operations, use a potting mix that contains some loam, but it should still be very much on the peaty side. Warm, moist and shaded conditions are essential if leaves are to retain their texture and brightness. Watering requires some care; plants must be moist at all times, but not saturated, especially in winter.

Take care
Mealy bug can weaken growth. 9♦

Aglaonema pseudobracteatum

(Golden evergreen)
- Light shade
- Temp: 18-21°C (65-70°F)
- Keep moist

A demanding plant, best suited to the experienced grower; the principal difficulty is the high temperature, which must be maintained. A height of 1m (39in) is not unusual in mature specimens. Leaf perimeter is green with a centre of whitish yellow.

New plants are propagated from top sections of stems with three sound leaves attached. Severed ends are allowed to dry for a few hours before being treated with rooting powder; plant in peaty mixture in small pots, and plunge in moist peat in a heated propagating case; to ensure success the temperature should be around 21°C (70°F). When potting cuttings for growing on, put three cuttings in a 13cm (5in) pot, using a potting mixture with a percentage of loam.

These plants are not much troubled by pests, but mealy bugs are sometimes found where the leaf stalks curl round the main stem. In this situation, thorough saturation with liquid insecticide will be needed.

Take care
Ensure adequate temperature. 10◆

Alocasia indica
- Light shade
- Temp: 18-24°C (65-75°F)
- Keep moist

One of the more exotic and temperamental members of the Araceae family. There are numerous cultivars, all with exotic velvety appearance and arrow-shaped leaves.

Their most important needs are for a temperature of around 24°C (75°F) and for a humid atmosphere. The soil in the pot must be kept moist at all times, and it is essential that the surrounding atmosphere is also moist; this will mean placing the plant on a large tray filled with gravel, which should be kept permanently wet. The tray can contain water, but the level should never be up to the surface of the pebbles so that the plant pot is actually standing in water. Plants allowed to stand in water become waterlogged, and will rot and die. Feeding is not important, but it will do no harm if liquid fertilizer is given periodically.

Take care
Keep plants out of draughts and away from hot radiators. 10◆

Alpinia sanderae
(Silver ginger)
- **Light shade**
- **Temp: 18-24°C (65-75°F)**
- **Avoid overwatering in winter**

One of the many ornamental members of the ginger family, Zingiberaceae, but at present they are generally in short supply. The ginger plant discussed here has highly coloured, upright stems of silver and green foliage, but is made very limited use of as a houseplant.

One of the problems is that it is slow to propagate, as one has to wait for plants to mature and then to divide up the clumps into smaller sections in order to produce additional plants; this is too slow for the commercial grower, who, on account of high energy costs, must have plants that can be put through his greenhouses in the shortest possible time.

To do well indoors, *A. sanderae* will need a minimum temperature of 18°C (65°F). It will also need careful watering and must never remain saturated for long, especially in winter. Feed in frequent weak doses rather than occasional heavy ones, and not in winter.

Take care
Avoid cold and wetness in winter. 11♦

Ananas bracteatus striatus
(Ivory pineapple)
- **Good light**
- **Temp: 13-18°C (55-65°F)**
- **Keep on dry side**

The best of the South American bromeliads, the green form of which, *A. comosus*, is the pineapple of commerce. There is also a white variegated form, also known as the ivory pineapple.

In good light the natural cream colouring of the foliage will be a much better colour, but one should avoid very strong sunlight that is magnified by clear glass. Wet root conditions that offer little drying out will also be harmful. Feed occasionally but avoid overdoing it. New plants can be produced by pulling offsets from mature plants and potting them individually in a mixture containing leaf mould and peat. In reasonable conditions plants can be expected to develop small pineapples in about three years; although highly decorative, these tend to be woody and inedible. However, as pineapples are developing, the central part of the plant around the base of the leaves will change to a brilliant reddish pink.

Take care
Avoid the spined leaf margins. 12♦

Anthurium crystallinum
- **Light shade**
- **Temp: 18-24°C (65-75°F)**
- **Moist atmosphere**

This plant is among the more temperamental foliage plants. It does produce a flower, but this is in fact a thin rat's tail. However, the rat's tail has the important function of producing seed, from which new plants can be raised relatively easily in a high temperature. The patterned, heart-shaped leaves are very large and spectacular and usually have to be supported if they are to show to their best advantage.

High temperature, lightly shaded location and humid atmosphere are their principal needs. Roots should at no time dry out. Regular feeding will maintain foliage in brighter colour and better condition. Potting mixture containing a percentage of loam should be used and the pot should be provided with drainage material. Although plants must not dry at their roots, it is essential that water should drain away freely.

Pests are not a problem. Avoid handling, or cleaning the leaves with chemical concoctions.

Take care
Maintain high humidity. 13♦

Aralia elegantissima
(False aralia)
- **Light shade**
- **Temp: 18-21°C (65-70°F)**
- **Keep moist**

Also known as *Dizygotheca elegantissima*, this is one of the most attractive of the purely foliage plants, having dark green, almost black, colouring to its leaves. Graceful leaves radiate from stiff, upright stems that will attain a height of about 3m (10ft). As the plant ages it loses its delicate foliage and produces leaves that are much larger and coarser in appearance. One can remove the upper section of stem, and new growth will revert to the original delicate appearance.

Warm conditions with no drop in temperature are important; water thoroughly, soaking the soil, and allow it to dry reasonably before repeating. Feed in spring and summer, less in winter.

Mealy bug can be treated with a liquid insecticide; affected areas should be thoroughly saturated with the spray. Root mealy bugs can be seen as a whitish powder around the roots; to clear these, liquid insecticide should be watered in.

Take care
Avoid fluctuating temperatures. 13♦

Aralia sieboldii
(Castor oil plant)
- **Light shade**
- **Temp: 7-13°C (45-55°F)**
- **Water and feed well**

Also known as *Fatsia japonica*. Besides being an excellent indoor plant it is hardy out of doors, and will develop into a large shrub.

The large fingered leaves have a deceptively tough appearance, as this plant can very easily be damaged by chemicals for the cleaning of foliage plants. They will also be scorched by the sun if placed too close to clear glass. In the first two or three years plants will require annual potting on until they are in 20 or 25cm (8 or 10in) pots. It then becomes impractical in the average home to advance them to larger containers, and it is important to ensure that they are regularly and adequately fed. New plants can be raised from seed sown in peaty mixture in a warm propagator in the spring.

Red spider can be troublesome in hot, dry conditions; a sign of their presence is pale brown patches on leaves. Use insecticide to treat reverse side of leaves thoroughly.

Take care
Avoid hot and dry conditions. 14♦

Araucaria excelsa
(Norfolk Island pine)
- **Light shade**
- **Temp: 13-18°C (55-65°F)**
- **Provide ample space**

A majestic tropical tree that originates from New Zealand. It is a marvellous foliage plant when carefully treated and not subjected to very high temperatures, which can be debilitating. Hot conditions cause normally turgid foliage to droop and become very thin. These elegant plants are best suited to important and spacious locations that will allow full development.

During early development plants should be allowed to fill their pots with roots before being potted on into slightly larger containers, using a loam-based potting mixture. When going into their final pots of 20-25cm (8-10in) diameter, the amount of loam should be increased to encourage slower but firmer growth. New plants can be raised from seed, but it is better to purchase small plants and grow them on.

Few pests trouble these pines, but excessive watering, especially in poor light, will cause browning and eventual loss of needles.

Take care
Avoid overpotting of young plants. 14♦

Ardisia crispa (A. crenulata)
(Coral berry)
- **Light shade**
- **Temp: 16-21°C (60-70°F)**
- **Keep moist and fed**

Although flowers are produced, the main attractions of the coral berry are the glossy green crenellated leaves and the long-lasting berries. It grows very slowly, and plants take several years to attain the maximum height of around 90cm (3ft). A stiff, upright central stem carries the woody branches, which will always be neat.

Offer a lightly shaded location for best results, and at no time be tempted to water excessively. Slow-growing plants of this kind are best kept on the dry side, particularly in winter. It is also important not to be too heavy-handed when feeding, and it should be discontinued altogether in winter. Plants with a slow growth rate are better grown in pots that are on the small side, and soil with a good percentage of loam must be used, as plants will quickly deteriorate in peat mixtures. Cuttings of firm young shoots can be taken in spring and rooted in peat at a temperature of not less than 21°C (70°F) to produce new plants.

Take care
Never overwater in winter. 15♦

Arundinaria
(Bamboo)
- **Good light**
- **Temp: 10-18°C (50-65°F)**
- **Keep moist and fed**

There are numerous varieties, some very vigorous, such as *A. gigantea* (common name, cane reed), others, such as *A. vagans*, neat and compact. These are ideal for cooler locations where there is reasonable light. In time the plants will form into bold groups of congested stems that completely fill the pots in which they are growing.

As plants increase in size they will generally require a greater amount of water, and feeding will have to be stepped up. The time will also come when plants have to be put into larger containers, and one should use a mixture containing a good amount of loam. As an alternative to potting the complete clump one can use a fork and spade to chop the clump up into smaller sections, which in turn can be potted up as individual plants. At all stages of growth plants will need ample watering and feeding, with winter being the only time when one should ease up on both.

Take care
Divide older plants periodically.

23

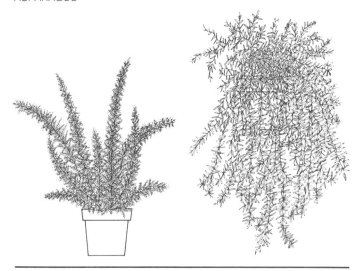

Asparagus meyerii
(Plume asparagus)
- Good light, no sun
- Temp: 13-18°C (55-65°F)
- Keep moist, less in winter

Although frequently referred to as ferns, these belong to the lily family. Not a common houseplant, *A. meyerii* is among the most elegant of indoor plants. As the common name suggests, the foliage forms pale green cylindrical plumes on stiff stems that may attain a length of 60cm (2ft). Growth forms in stout clumps and springs from soil level.

It is important when potting that the plants should be placed centrally in the new container. A loam-based potting mixture should be used to keep plants in good fettle. Once established in their pots a regular feeding schedule must be followed, especially during the spring and summer months. Plants fare better if rain water is used in preference to tap water. And when watering the soil do it thoroughly, with surplus water being clearly seen to drain through the holes in the bottom of the pot. It is then important to allow a reasonable drying-out period before further water is given. Less water is required in winter.

Take care
Never use very peaty soil. 15♦

Asparagus sprengeri
(Asparagus fern)
- Good light, no sun
- Temp: 13-18°C (55-65°F)
- Water and feed well

Though the common name suggests a fern, this is a member of the lily family. One of the most vigorous and useful of all the many fine foliage plants, it is especially effective when grown in a hanging basket.

New plants can be raised from seed sown in spring, or one can divide mature plants at almost any time of year. Before division, ensure that the soil is thoroughly wetted. As with potting on, divided pieces should be planted in pots that give the roots space, and the potting mixture must contain a reasonable amount of loam. In order to keep the lush green colouring it is important that well-rooted plants should be fed regularly. Feeding with weak liquid fertilizer at every watering is often more satisfactory than giving plants occasional heavy doses. Although plants will appreciate good light it is important to protect them from direct sun. Also, in hot, dry conditions it will help if foliage is periodically sprayed over with water.

Take care
Avoid cold winter locations.

Aspidistra elatior
(Cast iron plant)
- **Light shade**
- **Temp: 13-18°C (55-65°F)**
- **Keep moist**

Popular since Victorian times, when it acquired its common name on account of its ability to withstand trying conditions. The aspidistra has been around for a very long time and there are plants alive today with a known history that goes back for over a century. A tough plant, but – like almost all such plants – the aspidistra will be much better if reasonably agreeable conditions are provided, rather than a very spartan environment that will result in the plant surviving and little else.

Reasonable light, evenly moist conditions that avoid extremes, with occasional feeding once established, will usually produce plants that are fresh and lush and much more attractive. When potting on, use a properly prepared mixture of soil that contains a good percentage of loam. Any good fertilizer will suit well-rooted plants.

The apparently tough leaves are very sensitive to the use of cleaning chemicals, and to household cleaning chemicals in general.

Take care
Never use chemicals on the foliage.

Asplenium nidus avis
(Bird's nest fern)
- **Shade**
- **Temp: 18-24°C (65-75°F)**
- **Moist roots and surroundings**

As small plants these are not very exciting, but once they have been advanced to pot sizes of around 18cm (7in) they have few equals. But the growing of these plants to perfection is one of the more difficult exercises in horticulture.
Surrounding objects touching tender leaves will almost certainly cause irreparable damage, as will spraying foliage with unsuitable chemicals, or the presence of slugs.

Leaves can be kept in good order if a temperature of around 21°C (70°F) is maintained and plants enjoy good light but not direct sun. Open, peaty mixture is needed when potting, and water applied to the top of the soil should immediately flow through. Frequent feeding of established plants with weak fertilizer is preferred to infrequent heavier doses. Keep soil moist.

Scale insects can be seen as dark brown or flesh-coloured spots adhering to the area around the midrib of the leaf. These can be sponged off with malathion.

Take care
Never handle young foliage. 16♦

Aucuba japonica variegata
(Spotted laurel)
- **Good light**
- **Temp: 7-13°C (45-55°F)**
- **Avoid summer drying out**

An old-established plant that will tolerate varied conditions, but prefers to grow in cool conditions. This is one of the few plants that do well in a draughty hallway. And it has the bonus of fairly colourful foliage.

New plants are little trouble to propagate, and one should remove the top section of the stem with about four sound leaves attached, and insert in a peaty mixture. Putting the pot with its cutting in a heated propagator will stimulate rooting, as will the use of rooting powder or liquid. Once rooted, transfer the young plant to a slightly larger pot, using a loam-based potting soil.

While plants are in active growth they should be watered freely and fed regularly; during the winter months water sparingly and discontinue feeding. Older plants that are losing their appearance can be pruned to shape in spring. During the summer, aucubas make excellent plants for the patio.

Take care
Avoid wet winter conditions.16♦

Beaucarnea recurvata
(Ponytail plant)
- **Light shade**
- **Temp: 10-21°C (50-70°F)**
- **Water well in summer**

A peculiar plant that people either love or hate. Leaves are narrow, green and recurving. Small plants produce neat, firm bulbs at the base of their stems, the bulbs changing into more grotesque shapes as the plant ages. Because of its odd spreading habit of growth it is used more as an individual plant than as one of a group of plants.

New plants can be raised from seed sown in peat in warm conditions at almost any time of the year. Pot the resultant seedlings into small pots of peat initially, and into loam-based compost when they are of sufficient size. As an alternative to seed, new plants can be grown from the small bulbils that develop around the base of the parent.

The plant puts up with much ill-treatment provided the soil in its pot is not allowed to remain permanently saturated. Once established, plants respond to regular feeding while in active growth; none in winter.

Take care
Avoid cold and wetness in winter.

Begonia masoniana
(Iron cross begonia)
- **Light shade**
- **Temp: 16-21°C (60-70°F)**
- **Keep dry in winter**

Begonia rex
(Fan plant)
- **Light shade**
- **Temp: 16-21°C (60-70°F)**
- **Keep on the dry side in winter**

This fine plant grows to splendid size if given reasonable care. The rough-surfaced leaves are a brownish green in colour and have a very distinctive cross that covers the greater part of the centre of the leaf and radiates from the area where the petiole is joined. This marking resembles the German Iron Cross.

During the spring and summer months it will be found that plants grow at reasonable pace if given a warm room, moist root conditions, and weak liquid fertilizer with each watering. Plants that have filled their existing pots with roots can be potted on at any time during the summer, using a loam-based potting mixture and shallow pots. Over the winter months loss of some lower leaves will be almost inevitable, but provided the soil is kept on the dry side during this time the plant will remain in better condition and will grow away with fresh leaves in the spring.

Take care
Inspect for winter rot. 33♦

These rank among the finest foliage plants, with all shades of colouring and intricate leaf patterns. Those with smaller leaves are generally easier to care for indoors.

To propagate, firm, mature leaves are removed from the plant and most of the leaf stalk is removed before a series of cuts are made through the thick veins on the underside of the leaf. The leaf is then placed underside down on moist peat (in either boxes or shallow pans) and a few pebbles are placed on top of the leaf, to keep it in contact with the moist peat. Temperatures in the region of 21°C (70°F) are required, and a propagating case. Alternatively, the leaf can be cut into squares of about 5cm (2in), and the pieces placed on moist peat.

When purchased these plants are often in pots that are much too small; repot the plant into a larger container without delay, using peaty compost.

Take care
In close conditions look out for signs of mildew developing. 33♦

Caladium candidum
(Angels' wings)
- **Light shade**
- **Temp: 18-24°C (65-75°F)**
- **Wet in summer, dry in winter**

This is possibly the most delicately beautiful of all the purely foliage plants. The leaves are heart-shaped, almost as broad as they are long, and have a kind of translucent whiteness. Across the white surface there are attractive heavy green veins.

Care is required when handling, but the very delicate appearance is deceptive, as they have a rubbery quality. When watering it is essential that the soil is soaked, and never allowed to dry out at any time during the growing season. Growth will be active from early spring to the autumn, when foliage will take on a tired appearance, and this is a sign that watering should be gradually reduced until the soil is bone dry. In this condition the tuber in its pot is stored until the following spring, when new growth appears; provide a storage temperature of around 16°C (60°F). In the early spring the soil should be moistened and the plant placed in a temperature of around 24°C (75°F) to stimulate new growth.

Take care
Provide adequate storage warmth.

Caladium hybrids
(Angels' wings)
- **Light shade**
- **Temp: 18-24°C (65-75°F)**
- **Keep moist when in leaf**

There is a wide variety of these hybrids, all in need of some cosseting if they are to succeed. Adequate temperature is essential, and they are sensitive to the effects of bright sun through clear glass.

When potting it is important to use a high proportion of peat that will drain freely. Repot over-wintered tubers soon after they have produced their first new growth. Old soil should be teased gently away, care being taken not to damage any new roots that may be forming. Rather than transfer plants to very large pots it is better, having removed much of the old soil, to repot the plant into the same container using fresh mixture.

Leaves of these plants will not tolerate any cleaning. When buying plants, get them from a reliable retailer with heated premises, as cold conditions for only a short time can be fatal. Although arum-type flowers are produced, these are unattractive and should be removed.

Take care
Provide adequate storage warmth. 34

Calathea makoyana
(Peacock plant)
- Shade
- Temp: 18-24°C (65-75°F)
- Keep moist and fed

Oval-shaped, paper-thin leaves are carried on petioles that may be as much as 60cm (2ft) long, and are intricately patterned. The peacock plant is of a delicate nature; it will rapidly succumb if the temperature is not to its liking. And it must at no time be exposed to direct sunlight, or shrivelling of leaves will occur.

Small plants are seldom offered for sale. It is usual for the specialist grower to raise plants in very warm beds of peat in the greenhouse; when plants are well established they are potted up into 18cm (7in) pots. For all potting operations a very peaty and open mixture containing some coarse leaf mould will be essential. And following potting it will be necessary to ensure that the soil remains just moist, but never becomes saturated for long periods.

Pests are seldom a problem, but established plants have to be fed with weak liquid fertilizer weekly from spring to autumn.

Take care
Protect from direct sunlight.34♦

Calathea oppen-heimiana tricolor
- Light shade
- Temp: 16-21°C (60-70°F)
- Water/feed mainly in summer

This is much easier to manage than almost any of the other calatheas. The leaves, on long petioles, are produced at soil level and radiate from the centre of the pot, forming compact and low-growing plants. Background colouring is a very dark green with streaks of white and pink attractively dispersed around the centre of the leaves.

Plants have to be divided in order to be increased. Although the commercial grower may find it slow to build up large stocks of these plants, they are very simple for the average indoor plantsman to cope with. Water the soil well and remove the plant from its pot before proceeding to split the clump of roots as one would divide a clump of herbaceous plants in the garden. At all potting stages use a proprietary houseplant potting mixture with a little loam added. Offer plants reasonable light and protection from direct sunlight, and always avoid excessive watering.

Take care
Avoid frequent use of chemicals.35♦

Calathea ornata
- Shade
- Temp: 18-24°C (65-75°F)
- Needs moist soil and atmosphere

The calatheas almost all present a challenge. Adequate temperature, shade and moist surroundings are their principal needs, but moist surroundings should not be confused with totally saturated soil. In fact, the roots should not remain excessively wet for long periods, but it is important to mist the foliage and the area surrounding the plant at regular intervals.

In its junior stages of growth, *C. ornata* produces oval-shaped leaves attractively marked with very fine pink lines on a green background. As the plant ages the lines become whiter, and in older plants are not always present. The leaves are paper-thin, and deep purple underneath. Feeding should be done at each watering, giving very weak dosage, with none in winter. Tepid rain water is better than cold tap water. Place plants on gravel or similar moisture-retaining surface, or put pots into a larger container filled with damp peat.

Take care
Never expose to bright sun.

Calathea picturata
- Shade
- Temp: 18-24°C (65-75°F)
- Keep moist

Oval-shaped leaves some 15cm (6in) long are carried on short petioles that are closely grouped at soil level, producing a plant of neat and compact appearance. The margin of each leaf is green and the centre is a striking silver-grey in colour; the reverse is maroon. As with all calatheas, bright direct sunlight will quickly kill them as leaves begin to shrivel up. Calatheas are happier growing in the shade of bolder plants such as the more spreading types of philodendron, such as *P. bipinnatifidum*.

Cold draughts – and cold conditions generally – must be avoided, and if possible one should provide a moist atmosphere around the plant; this is often best achieved by placing plants in a container that includes a selection of other plants. Large containers are now freely available for making plant arrangements in. Fill a container with moist peat into which the plant pot is plunged to its rim.

Take care
Keep moist and warm.

Calathea zebrina
(Zebra plant)
● Shade
● Temp: 18-24°C (65-75°F)
● Keep moist and fed

This incredibly beautiful foliage plant will test the skills of anyone. The bold leaves are a deep velvety green with prominent patches of deeper colouring. Maximum height of around 90cm (3ft) may be attained in a well-heated greenhouse where plants are tended with professional care.

It will be fatal to allow this plant to stand in a position exposed to full sunlight for even the shortest space of time. It is remarkable that this plant with its highly coloured exotic appearance should produce such beautiful leaves while growing in shaded locations. But *C. zebrina* always does very much better when placed under and in the shade of taller plants such as ficus and philodendrons, which offer a dark canopy of leaves. When watering, use tepid water and be sure that the soil is thoroughly soaked each time; but allow a drying-out period between waterings. Feed while new leaves are growing.

Take care
Avoid draughts and direct sun. 35♦

Carex morrowii variegata
(Japanese sedge)
● Light shade
● Temp: 7-18°C (45-65°F)
● Keep moist and fed

One of the most durable potted plants of them all, putting up with a wide variation of temperatures. It will also adapt reasonably well to erratic watering and feeding neglect, but in extreme conditions there is a likelihood of leaf turning brown. The narrow, arching grassy leaves are white-striped and about 30cm (12in) long, and form neat clusters.

To do well, this plant should be well watered and allowed to dry a little before repeating. Feeding should be done during spring and summer, not at other times. When bushy clumps of leaves have formed, pot plants on into slightly larger containers using a mixture containing some loam.

Propagation is very simple: water the pot, remove the plant, then divide the clump into smaller sections and pot the pieces individually into small pots to begin with, repotting them as they become large enough. Very hot conditions will be detrimental; cool and light are best.

Take care
Divide older clumps periodically.

Ceropegia woodii
(Hearts entangled)
- **Suspend in good light**
- **Temp: 13-18°C (55-65°F)**
- **Moist, but dry in winter**

With the current fashion for hanging plants of all kinds this is the ideal plant to try, as it is so different from almost all other potted plants. Small, fleshy heart-shaped leaves are attached to wiry stems that hang perpendicularly from the plant. *C. woodii* is a hanging plant with no desire whatsoever to climb or do anything different. The leaves are mottled and grey-green in colour and the flowers are pink and tubular.

The common name of 'hearts entangled' comes from the manner in which the foliage twines around itself when the plants are growing actively. There is also the additional fascination of the gnarled bulbous growths that appear at soil level and along the stems of the plant, from which new growth sprouts. Indeed, the bulbils with growth attached can be used to propagate fresh plants, or they can be raised from cuttings.

When planting hanging containers it is advisable to propagate a batch of plants and to put five or so into each.

Take care
Avoid overwet winter conditions. 37♦

Chlorophytum comosum variegatum
(Spider plant; St. Bernard's lily)
- **Airy, good light**
- **Temp: 10-16°C (50-60°F)**
- **Frequent feeding**

Like privet hedges in the garden the chlorophytums of the houseplant world appear to be everywhere. Yet they are not always as bright and healthy as their ease of culture would suggest they should be – in fact, many are extremely poor specimens. This may be due to the fact that owners feel that they are so easy to grow that they don't have to bother at all.

Give the chlorophytum good light to prevent it becoming thin and straggly, and keep it moist at all times, especially during summer.

The most important need of all, and the one most neglected, is that of feeding, and feeding the spider plant means giving it very much more than the average indoor plant. Frequent potting on is also essential, and this could be necessary twice a year for vigorous plants. Spider plants produce large fleshy roots and quickly become starved if not supplied with sufficient nourishment. Use a loam-based potting mixture.

Take care
Aphids cause blotched leaves. 36♦

32

Above: **Begonia masoniana**
*Distinctive brown markings in the
centre of the leaf give this plant the
apt common name of iron cross
begonia. Plants develop into a neat,
rounded shape as they age. Rough
textured foliage makes cleaning
impossible other than by dusting
with a soft brush.* 27♦

Right: **Begonia rex**
*Wealth of colour in the foliage and
intricate leaf patterns place these
plants among the elite of
houseplants. Plants vary in their
ease of culture, with smaller-leaved,
more compact types being generally
easier to raise. Leaves are borne on
rhizomatous stems.* 27♦

Above: **Caladium hybrid**
*Supreme foliage plants that have
leaves thin enough to be translucent
in some varieties. Growth dies down
in the autumn.* 28♦

Left: **Calathea makoyana**
*The peacock plant has large, oval-
shaped leaves that are intricately
patterned and paper thin. Stout leaf
stalks spring from soil level.* 29♦

Top right: **Calathea zebrina**
*The leaves of this plant have a
velvety texture, and are among the
most beautiful of all foliage plants.
Warmth and shade essential.* 31♦

Right: **Calathea oppenheimiana
tricolor**
*Perhaps the easiest of the calatheas
to care for. Colouring varies; better
examples have more pink.* 29♦

Above: **Chlorophytum comosum variegatum**
The familiar spider plant develops natural plantlets that can be used for propagating new plants. 32♦

Right: **Ceropegia woodii**
Natural trailing plants with grey-coloured heart-shaped leaves that have a succulent, puffed up appearance. 32♦

Below: **Cissus discolor**
The aristocrat of the decorative pot-grown vines. It has a natural climbing habit and does best in warm, shaded and moist conditions. 49♦

Above:
Codiaeum 'Eugene Drapps'
*By far the best yellow-coloured of
the commonly named Joseph's coat
plants. Grow in good light.* 51▸

Left: **Cocos weddelliana**
*The best of the finer foliaged palms,
and a slow growing plant that will
seldom outgrow its allotted space.
With age a basal trunk will form.* 50▸

Right: **Codiaeum hybrids**
*Codiaeums in general are among the
most highly coloured of all foliage
plants, but must have ample light if
they are not to revert to green.* 50▸

Above: **Coleus**
Easily cared for and in many brilliant colours that are seen at their best when grown in good light. 51♦

Top right: **Cryptanthus bromelioides tricolor**
This earth star has an extended growth habit and beautiful colour. 53♦

Right: **Cryptanthus 'Foster's Favourite'**
The stiff, unbending leaves of this fine bromeliad form a star shape. 53♦

Below:
Columnea banksii variegata
A fine trailing plant with small, plump, green-and-white leaves. 52♦

Above: **Cyperus alternifolius**
*Insignificant green leaves occur at
the base of stately stems 1.5-2.1m
(5-7ft) tall, from which sprout
umbrella-like canopies of growth.
Much water needed.* 54♦

Left: **Cryptanthus bromelioides 'It'**
*Small, star-shaped radiating growth
is neat and compact, making plants
ideal for small plant gardens in
bottles. Fascinating pink colour.* 52♦

Below: **Cyrtomium falcatum**
*With dark green, holly-like foliage
(but with no spines), the holly fern is
a long-established favourite. A
robust plant for shady places.* 55♦

Above:
Dichorisandra albo-lineata
Tall-growing plants of the tradescantia tribe with green-and-white variegation that need good light to thrive. 56♦

Left: **Dieffenbachia amoena**
One of the most majestic of the dumb canes, growing to a height of 150cm (5ft) and 120cm (4ft) across. Bold green leaves have tracery of white in their central areas. 57♦

Right: **Dieffenbachia camilla**
Introduced in the late 1970s and one of the finest of all the many dieffenbachias. The green-margined leaf is almost entirely cream. 57♦

Above: **Dieffenbachia picta**
*A well-established plant of graceful
appearance with attractive pale
green speckled foliage.* 58♦

Left: **Dieffenbachia exotica**
*The forerunner of the more compact
dumb canes. It produces young
growth at the base of the parent stem
to give the plant a much fuller
appearance.* 58♦

Right:
Dieffenbachia 'Tropic Snow'
*Bold foliage plants with stout green-
and-white leaves. Needs warm,
moist, shady conditions.* 59♦

Above: **Dionaea muscipula**
The well-known Venus's fly trap is very difficult to care for, but has the fascinating ability of being able to catch flies in its sensitive leaves. 59♦

Below: **Dracaena deremensis 'Warneckii'**
A stately plant with grey-green and white striped foliage that grows to a height of 2.4-3m (8-10ft). 60♦

Cissus antarctica
(Kangaroo vine)
- **Light shade**
- **Temp: 13-18°C (55-65°F)**
- **Keep moist**

As the common name suggests, these plants originate from Australia. The mid-green leaves have toothed margins and are seen at their best when plants are allowed to climb against a framework or wall. In favourable conditions stems will add yards of growth, but trimming back to shape can be undertaken at any time of year, so there is no possibility of them out-growing their welcome. These are useful plants for the more difficult and possibly darker location indoors.

Cuttings consisting of two firm leaves with a piece of main stem attached will root at any time if a temperature of around 18-21°C (65-70°F) can be maintained; treat cuttings with a rooting powder. It is advisable to put several cuttings in one pot when they are removed from the propagator.

Peat compost will suit them fine, but it is essential that feeding is not neglected when plants are growing in this sort of mixture.

Take care
Dry soil will cause leaf-loss.

Cissus discolor
(Begonia vine)
- **Light shade**
- **Temp: 18-24°C (65-75°F)**
- **Keep moist and fed**

This most beautiful climbing foliage plant has maroon undersides, and an upper leaf surface with a mixture of silver, red, green and other colours. Plants climb by means of clinging tendrils if given some support; to prevent gaps appearing as plants extend, pin some of the straying shoots down the stem.

A dry atmosphere can result in shrivelling of the leaves, as will exposure to bright sun; and very dry soil conditions also cause leaf problems. It seems necessary to renew older plants periodically rather than allow them to become straggly. Cuttings prepared from mature, firm leaves with stem attached will root in a temperature of 21°C (70°F) if put into small pots filled with moist peat. A closed propagating case and treating cuttings with rooting powder will also speed the process. Once rooted, cuttings should be potted into slightly larger pots using peaty mixture, and the soil thereafter kept moist but not waterlogged.

Take care
Avoid bright sun. 36♦

49

Cocos weddelliana
(Weddell palm)
- **Light shade**
- **Temp: 16-21°C (60-70°F)**
- **Keep moist and fed**

Possibly the most beautiful and delicate of all the many palms offered for sale. However, being slow growing it is seen less often these days, as the commercial grower concentrates his efforts on palms that attain saleable size in a shorter time. One choice specimen of *C. weddelliana* is over 60 years old, with many fine stems reaching a height of some 3m (10ft).

A position out of direct sunlight is advised but one should not put the plant in the darkest corner, as reasonable light is essential to its well-being. Established plants can be fed at every watering with weak liquid fertilizer, with less being given – perhaps none at all – in winter. Some chemicals are harmful, so one should check suitability with the supplier before applying.

Its principal enemy is red spider mite. These mites cause pale discolouration of the foliage and are mostly found on the undersides of leaves.

Take care
Check regularly for red spider. 38♦

Codiaeum hybrids
(Joseph's coat)
- **Good light**
- **Temp: 16-21°C (60-70°F)**
- **Feed and water well**

Also known as crotons, these plants are among the most colourful of all foliage plants, as the common name suggests.

Full light, with protection from the strongest sunlight, is essential if plants are to retain their bright colouring. In poor light, new growth becomes thin and poor, and colouring is less brilliant. Besides light there is a need for reasonable temperature, without which shedding of lower leaves will be inevitable. Healthy plants that are producing new leaves will require to be kept moist with regular watering, but it is important that the soil should be well drained. Frequent feeding is necessary, though less is needed in winter. On account of vigorous top growth, there will be a mass of roots in the pots of healthy plants. Large plants that seem out of proportion to their pots should be inspected in spring and summer. If well rooted they should be potted into larger pots using loam-based compost.

Take care
Check regularly for red spider.39♦

Codiaeum 'Eugene Drapps'

(Joseph's coat)
- **Good light**
- **Temp: 16-21°C (60-70°F)**
- **Feed and water well**

One of the queens of potted plants. The leaves are lance-shaped and almost entirely yellow in colour; only on closer inspection is it seen that there is also some green present.

New plants are grown from cuttings taken from the top section of the stem. Cuttings will have four or five leaves, and will be 15cm (6in) or more in length. A temperature in excess of 21°C (70°F) is needed to encourage rooting, and conditions should be close and moist. Once rooted in their peat propagating mixture, plants must be potted into loam-based compost as soon as they have made a reasonable amount of root. Once plants have got under way the top of the stem should be pinched out, to encourage the plant to branch.

In common with all codiaeums, this one will almost certainly attract red spider mites. These are difficult to detect on yellow foliage and a magnifying glass is usually necessary.

Take care
Keep moist, warm and light. 38♦

Coleus

(Flame nettle)
- **Good light**
- **Temp: 10-16°C (50-60°F)**
- **Keep moist and fed**

For little outlay the coleus offers more foliage colour than almost any other potted plant. Small plants can be purchased almost anywhere during the spring.

On getting plants home, if they are growing in small pots, advance them to pots a little larger in size. All the coleuses are hungry plants and any neglect with potting – or subsequently with feeding – will result in plants of much poorer quality. Full sun streaming through unprotected glass will usually be harmful, but these plants need plenty of light if they are to retain their colouring. Due to their light position it will be necessary to water plants frequently (every day, in some instances), and to ensure that the soil is thoroughly soaked each time. Better coloured plants can be retained from one year to the next; but it is better to take cuttings from these in late summer and to dispose of the often overgrown larger plant.

Take care
Provide good light for fine colour. 40♦

Columnea banksii variegata
(Variegated goldfish plant)
- **Light shade**
- **Temp: 16-21°C (60-70°F)**
- **Keep moist in summer**

The columneas are generally free-flowering plants, but the variegated form of *C. banksii* can be included among foliage plants, as it rarely produces flowers. The foliage is highly variegated, slow growing, and pendulous. The leaves are plump and fleshy, and attached to slender dropping stems; plants are seen at their best when suspended in a basket or hanging pot.

Cuttings are more difficult to root than the green forms of columnea. Short sections of stem with the lower leaves removed are best for propagating; treat with rooting powder before the cuttings, five to seven in small pots, are inserted in a peat and sand mixture. A temperature of at least 21°C (70°F) is necessary and a propagator will be a great advantage. Due to the very slow rate of growth, it is necessary to allow the soil to dry reasonably between waterings. Feed with weak fertilizer, but never overdo it.

Take care
Keep reasonably warm. 40♦

Cryptanthus bromelioides 'It'
(Earth star)
- **Light shade**
- **Temp: 16-21°C (60-70°F)**
- **Keep on dry side**

A comparatively recent introduction that resembles *C. tricolor,* but is of much bolder pink and is more attractive, although individual plants vary in brightness of colour. The new variety also grows closer to the pot. The leaves are stiffer in appearance, begin with a thick base attached to a short main stem, and taper to a point.

Cryptanthuses, like all bromeliads, require to be potted into a very open, free-draining mixture. One suggestion is to prepare a mixture of coarse leaf mould and a peaty houseplant potting mixture and to pot the plants in this, using small containers. Treated tree bark that is not too coarse may be used as a substitute for leaf mould. Place a few pieces of broken pot in the bottom of the container before introducing the soil. When watering these plants it is important that they have a thorough soak and then be allowed to dry reasonably before more is given. Clean rain water will be ideal.

Take care
Avoid sodden root conditions. 42♦

Cryptanthus bromelioides tricolor
(Earth star)
- **Light shade**
- **Temp: 16-21°C (60-70°F)**
- **Keep on dry side**

The pink, green and white colouring of this plant can be spectacular in well-grown specimens, but they are not easy plants to care for. Although grouped with the other flatter-growing cryptanthuses under the same common name of earth star, these have a slightly different habit of growth. The centre of the plant tends to extend upwards, and new plant growth sprouts from the side of the parent rosette. If these side growths are left attached to the parent a full and handsome plant will in time develop; or they can be removed when of reasonable size by pulling them sideways; it is then simple to press the pieces into peaty mixture for them to produce roots.

Almost all cryptanthuses are terrestrial and are seen at their best when nestled in the crevices of an old tree stump, or surrounded by a few stones. *C. tricolor,* with its more open habit of growing, can also be effective in a hanging pot or basket.

Take care
Avoid wet and cold conditions. 41♦

Cryptanthus 'Foster's Favourite'
(Earth star)
- **Light shade**
- **Temp: 16-21°C (60-70°F)**
- **Avoid excessive watering**

Another splendid example from the fine bromeliad family from tropical South America. Named after a famous American nurseryman, this tends to be much larger than most cryptanthus plants and produces long leaves with a pheasant-feather pattern. The thick, fleshy leaves have the shape of a dagger blade and radiate from a short central stem.

In their natural habitat these plants grow on the floor of the forest among old tree stumps and boulders, so they are capable of withstanding rough treatment. But remember the old maxim – which applies to almost all indoor plants – that when low temperatures prevail or plants are likely to be exposed to trying conditions they will fare much better if kept on the dry side. In fact, no bromeliads will prosper if roots are confined to pots that are permanently saturated. An open potting mixture is essential so that water can drain through very freely.

Take care
Never overwater. 41♦

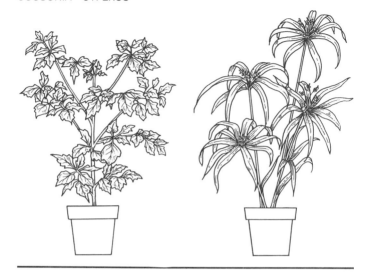

Cussonia spictata
- **Light shade**
- **Temp: 13-21°C (55-70°F)**
- **Keep moist and fed**

If obtainable, it will not be difficult to raise new plants from seed. Given moist peat in which to germinate and a temperature in the region of 21°C (70°F), seed will soon get under way. From the seedling stage a loam-based potting mixture will be best, and in the first year potting on of vigorous plants should not be neglected. By the end of their first year, have plants in 13cm (5in) pots; in the spring of the second year, pot them on into 18cm (7in) pots. In their third year, pot on into 25cm (10in) pots if plants are obviously vigorous.

At all stages of potting on of these very vigorous plants it is advisable to use loam-based potting mixture. Also, when plants are established in their pots it is essential that they should be fed with a balanced liquid fertilizer at least once each week except during the winter months. Less water is also needed during the winter, although it may be necessary to continue watering plants that are clearly growing and able to take up moisture.

Take care
Keep well nourished.

Cyperus alternifolius
(Umbrella plant)
- **Light shade**
- **Temp: 13-18°C (55-65°F)**
- **Wet conditions**

Of the two cyperus species occasionally offered for sale this one is the less suitable for indoor conditions on account of its height and its need for very high humidity. The narrow green leaves have little attraction, but green flowers produced on stems that may attain 1.8-2.4m (6-8ft) have a certain fascination. The tall stems of *C. alternifolius* provide an interesting feature at higher level when planting indoor water gardens.

When grown indoors these water-loving plants must be given all the water they require. Although it would be death to most houseplants, place the pot in a large saucer capable of holding a reasonable amount of water, and ensure that the water level is regularly topped up.

Established plants benefit from regular feeding in liquid or tablet form. Tablets pressed into the soil at the frequency recommended by the manufacturer will provide a continual source of nutrient and is one of the best methods of feeding.

Take care
Keep permanently wet. 43♦

Cyperus diffusus
(Umbrella plant)
- **Light shade**
- **Temp: 13-18°C (55-65°F)**
- **Wet conditions**

Flower stalks with their umbrella-like tops are produced in large numbers and attain around 60cm (2ft). The green leaves are not attractive, but the combination of leaves and flower stalks presents an attractive plant that will thrive in wet conditions.

Ideally, *C. diffusus* should stand in a large saucer that is kept permanently filled with water. The simplest way to raise new plants is to split up the clump of small plants into sections that can be easily accommodated in a 13cm (5in) pot. Use a compost that contains a good proportion of loam, and pot firmly so that the roots will hold together in the very wet conditions.

Few pests trouble these plants, but there may be the occasional mealy bug. These are mostly to be found around the flowers, and one should use a small firm paint brush that has been soaked in methylated spirits to remove them. Mealy bugs are white and powdery and enclose their young in a protective covering that resembles cotton wool.

Take care
Keep permanently wet.

Cyrtomium falcatum
(Holly fern)
- **Shade**
- **Temp: 16-21°C (60-70°F)**
- **Keep moist**

As the common name suggests, this fern's foliage has the appearance of holly, and is dark, glossy green in colour. Individual fronds will grow to some 60cm (2ft) in length when mature.

Suitable conditions are necessary for maximum success in fern propagation. But reasonable results can be obtained in the home if a heated propagator and moist, not saturated, conditions are available. Older leaves develop spores on the back; these have the appearance of a brownish rust that could well be mistaken for disease. When spores can be seen to fall like a fine dust when the leaf is tapped, the leaf can be removed and put in a paper bag in a warm place and left for a few days. The spores can then be sown on the surface of moist peat and placed in a propagator to germinate. They should be sown sparingly, as a dense mass of young plants will appear if conditions are right. When large enough to handle, these should be potted in peaty mixture.

Take care
Avoid direct sunlight. 43♦

Davallia canariensis

(Hare's foot fern)
- **Light shade**
- **Temp: 10-16°C (50-60°F)**
- **Moist in summer, drier in winter**

Besides being useful on the windowsill, these toughish ferns also make fine hanging plants. The fans of foliage are pale green and stiff, and are carried on firm stems.

New plants can be raised from ripe spores sown at any time in a temperature of not less than 21°C (70°F); the peat on which spores are sown should be kept moist. A simpler method is to divide the rhizomes of mature plants in spring, and to pot the small sections in pots filled with houseplant potting mixture containing a high proportion of peat.

While they are in active growth, keep plants moist; and during the less active months ensure that watering is not overdone. Established plants can be fed during spring and summer, but winter feeding should be avoided.

Be careful when contemplating the use of chemicals on these plants, as they can be very easily damaged: try the chemical on a small part of the plant first as a trial.

Take care
Avoid winter wetness.

Dichorisandra albo-lineata

- **Light shade**
- **Temp: 16-21°C (60-70°F)**
- **Keep moist and fed**

This member of the tradescantia family is also known as *Campelia zanonia albo-marginata.* Growing to a height of some 120cm (4ft) when confined to a pot, it produces lance-shaped leaves that are green and white in colour, edged with red. Stems are woody and plants are attractive enough, but they shed their lower leaves as they increase in height, which produces leafless stalks with rosettes of foliage at the top. Put them with other plants, so that they occupy the rear position with shorter plants in front.

Alternatively, the top section can be removed and rooted in warm conditions; when growing well it can be planted at the base of the parent plant to grow up and partly cover the bare stem. New growth will appear below where the cuttings were removed. Plants should be kept moist and warm, and when potting, loam-based mixture should be used. Plants can be fed while growing new leaves, but not in winter.

Take care
Avoid wetness and cold in winter. 44♦

Dieffenbachia amoena
(Dumb cane)
- **Light shade**
- **Temp: 18-24°C (65-75°F)**
- **Keep moist and fed**

This is possibly the largest of the dieffenbachias. The large, striking grey-green leaves with central colouring of speckled white and green will add much to any collection of indoor plants, but mature plants attain a height of 1.2-1.5m (4-5ft) with equal spread. However, stout stems can be cut out with a small saw. When carrying out any sort of work on dieffenbachias, though, gloves should be worn to prevent any sap getting onto one's skin. Even moving plants that have wet foliage may result in skin disorders. Also keep plants out of reach of children and pets. The common name of dumb cane derives from the fact that if the sap of the plant gets into one's mouth it will have unpleasant effects. Fortunately, such an occurrence is unlikely, as the sap has a very nasty odour.

Dieffenbachias belong to the same family of plants as the philodendrons, and respond to the same sort of conditions.

Take care
Never get sap onto your skin.

Dieffenbachia camilla
(Dumb cane)
- **Light shade**
- **Temp: 16-21°C (60-70°F)**
- **Keep moist and fed**

The beauty of this plant lies in the incredible colouring of the leaves, which have a green margin and a central area that is almost entirely creamy white. And anyone who knows their plants will be aware that areas of white in any leaf constitute a weakness that renders the plant vulnerable to leaf rot. But the thin marginal band of green seems to offer some form of protection, and this is in fact a reasonably easy plant.

With a maximum height around 60cm (2ft), it is much better suited to indoor conditions of today than most of the dieffenbachias available. Even as a small plant this one will have a natural tendency to produce basal shoots around the main plant stem, which gives a fuller and more attractive appearance. This plant is one of the indispensables when it comes to arranging plant displays. In groups indoors many moisture-loving plants will do much better if they are placed together in arrangements.

Take care
Never get sap onto your skin.45♦

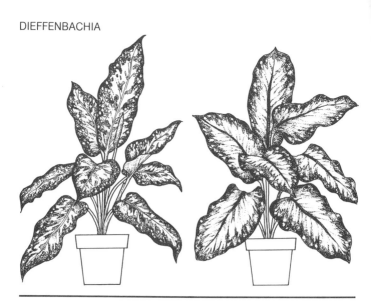

Dieffenbachia exotica
(Dumb cane)
● **Light shade**
● **Temp: 16-21°C (60-70°F)**
● **Keep moist and fed**

Dieffenbachia picta
(Dumb cane)
● **Light shade**
● **Temp: 18-24°C (65-75°F)**
● **Keep moist and fed**

The introduction of *D. exotica* within the past decade was something of a revolution as far as dieffenbachias were concerned. Previous plants of this kind were decidedly difficult subjects to grow at the nurseries, to transport, and to keep once they arrived at the home of the purchaser; they were also inclined to be too large for the average room of today.

D. exotica is a neat plant growing to a maximum of 60cm (2ft) – much more suitable for indoors – and with a much tougher constitution. It tolerates lower temperatures, and if not too wet does not seem to suffer. It produces clusters of young plants at the base of the parent stem, and can be propagated easily by removing the basal shoots and planting them separately in small pots filled with peat. Once rooted they should be potted in a peaty houseplant compost. Shoots can often be removed with roots attached, but gloves should be worn.

This is one of the traditional warm greenhouse plants that may have been found in many a Victorian conservatory at the turn of the century when exotic plants were all the rage. Not seen so frequently today, *D. picta* has speckled yellowish-green colouring and grows to a height of 90cm (3ft) when given proper care. If the top of the plant is removed when young, the plant will produce numerous side growths that will make it a more attractive shape. An effective display plant when carefully grown.

In common with all the many fine dieffenbachias these plants require warm and humid conditions. Permanently saturated soil must be avoided, but it is important that the pot is well watered with each application, and surplus water is seen to drain through the bottom of the pot. It is equally important that the soil should dry reasonably before further water is given.

Take care
Never get sap onto your skin.46♦

Take care
Avoid low temperatures.47♦

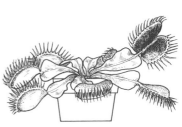

Dieffenbachia 'Tropic Snow'
(Dumb cane)
- **Light shade**
- **Temp: 18-24°C (65-75°F)**
- **Keep moist and fed**

This is a close relative of *D. amoena*, the difference being that the leaves of this plant are stiffer in appearance and have a greater area of white.

New plants are raised from cuttings, and these may be prepared either from the top section of the stem with two or more leaves attached, or from sections of thick stem that have no leaves whatsoever. Top sections are put into pots of peat at a temperature of 21°C (70°F). The stems are cut into sections 10cm (4in) long and laid on their sides in boxes of peat; it is important that the stem cutting should have a growth bud from which growth may in time develop.

Leaves of this plant are inclined to be brittle and are easily damaged if carelessly handled. There is also need for care when plant leaves are being cleaned: a supporting hand should be placed underneath the leaf as the upper area is wiped clean with a soft cloth or sponge. Do not use chemical cleaners too often.

Take care
Never get sap onto your skin.47♦

Dionaea muscipula
(Venus's fly trap)
- **Light shade**
- **Temp: 18-27°C (65-80°F)**
- **Moist atmosphere**

The Venus's fly trap is one of the most difficult of potted plants to care for indoors, but the appealing common name will ensure that it retains continued popularity.

Plants may be bought in pots in dormant stage or be acquired in leaf and growing in small pots covered by a plastic dome. The dome offers the plant some protection and helps to retain essential humidity around the plant while it is in transit, so making the dome-covered plant a much better buy. When caring for these plants adequate warmth and high humidity are essential.

When the leaves are touched, a mechanism within the plant induces the oval-shaped leaves to fold together. There are also long stiff hairs along the margins of the leaves; a fly, alighting on the leaf, will activate the mechanism and become trapped. The plant can digest the fly, and feeding flies and minute pieces of meat to the leaves is one way of nourishing the plant.

Take care
Humidity and warmth are essential. 48♦

Dracaena deremensis 'Bausei'

Dioscorea discolor
(Variegated yam)
- **Light shade**
- **Temp: 18-24°C (65-75°F)**
- **Keep moist when in leaf**

The heart-shaped leaves are maroon on the reverse; the upper surface is in many shades of dark and light green fusing together with silver-grey. The stems are thin and the species has a tendency to climb.

These plants are grown from potato-like tubers that are placed in 13cm (5in) pots filled with loam-based soil; peat would be quite unable to sustain them.

A temperature in the region of 21°C (70°F) is required to force the yams into growth, but once they start you can almost stand and watch them grow. These natural climbers will need a tall trellis for support.

The plant will die down in autumn, when tubers should be stored in their pots in a warm place. The following spring, all the old soil should be removed from around the tubers, and they should then be potted in a fresh mixture.

Ample watering and feeding will be needed while plants are growing, and they cannot abide low temperatures or bright sunlight.

Take care
Keep stored tubers warm and dry.

Dracaena deremensis
(Striped dracaena)
- **Light**
- **Temp: 16-21°C (60-70°F)**
- **Keep on the dry side**

There are numerous improved forms of this dracaena, all erect with broad, pointed leaves up to 60cm (2ft) long. The variations are mostly in leaf colour: *D. deremensis* Bausei has a dark green margin and glistening white centre; in *D. deremensis* Souvenir de Schriever the top-most rosette of leaves is bright yellow, but the leaves revert to the grey-green with white stripes of the parent plant as they age.

An unfortunate aspect of this type of dracaena is that they shed lower leaves as they increase in height, so that they take on a palm-like appearance with tufts of leaves at the top of otherwise bare stems. Although loss of lower leaves is a natural process, the incidence of dying and falling leaves will be aggravated by excessive watering. Water thoroughly, and then allow the soil to dry reasonably before repeating. These are hungry plants and will be in need of regular feeding, with loam-based soil recommended for potting on.

Take care
Never allow to become too wet. 48►

Dracaena fragrans 'Massangeana'

Dracaena fragrans
(Corn palm)
● **Light shade**
● **Temp: 18-24°C (65-75°F)**
● **Keep moist and fed**

The green-foliaged type is seldom offered for sale, but there are two important cultivars. The easiest to care for is *D. fragrans* 'Massangeana', which has broad mustard-coloured leaves attached to stout central stems; and presenting a little more difficulty there is *D. fragrans* 'Victoria' with brighter creamy-gold colouring.

As with most dracaenas there will be loss of lower leaves as plants increase in height, but plants eventually take on a stately, palm-like appearance.

Fortunately, few pests trouble these plants, but there is the occasional possibility of mealy bugs finding their way into the less accessible parts that lie between the base of the leaf and the stem of the plant. Prepare malathion solution and with the aid of a hand sprayer inject the insecticide down among the base of the leaves. As with all activities involving insecticides, wear rubber gloves and take all recommended precautions.

Take care
Feed established plants well.67♦

Dracaena godseffiana
(Gold dust dracaena)
● **Good light**
● **Temp: 16-21°C (60-70°F)**
● **Keep moist and fed**

Unlike most dracaenas, this one has rounded leaves attached to wiry stems that rarely attain a height of more than 90cm (3ft). The green form is not so attractive, but the cultivar *D. godseffiana* 'Florida Beauty' is a fine plant with yellow foliage interspersed with green.

As with all dracaenas, use a well-drained loam-based compost when potting on into larger containers. The comparatively low, spreading growth will be more suited to shallow containers. Put some drainage material in the bottom of the pot before the soil is introduced. Broken pieces of clay pot are ideal.

It is seldom necessary to use containers more than 18cm (7in) in diameter; but once plants are established in pots of this size, ensure that they get regular feeding. This usually means feeding about once a week while plants are in active growth, but in the winter only if fresh leaves are appearing and the plant is growing in very agreeable conditions.

Take care
Avoid excessive watering.

 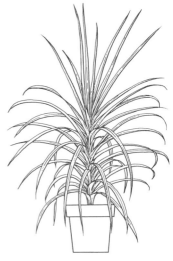

Dracaena marginata
(Silhouette plant)
● **Light shade**
● **Temp: 13-21°C (55-70°F)**
● **Keep on dry side**

D. marginata's dagger-shaped leaves have a reddish margin and are attached to firm upright whitish-grey stems. Among the easiest of indoor plants to care for, its only major objection is to excessive watering. Water plants well and allow them to dry out before repeating, and they will present few problems. Similar in habit is *D. marginata tricolor,* which has an attractive pink colouring but is a little more difficult to care for. See separate article for more details.

Both plants can grow to some 1.8-2.4m (6-8ft), but by pinching out the growing tip at a height of 90cm (3ft) it will be found that a plant with multiheads will result. This provides a more compact and neater plant for the average living room. Top sections root readily in a mixture of peat and sand if placed in a propagator at a temperature around 21°C (70°F). When potting on, use a loam-based mixture and pot firmly. Peaty mixtures are of little value to large plants.

Take care
Avoid saturated root conditions.

Dracaena marginata tricolor
(Variegated silhouette plant)
● **Good light**
● **Temp: 16-21°C (60-70°F)**
● **Avoid wet conditions**

This plant has a natural tendency to shed lower leaves as it increases in height. Nevertheless, it can be an elegant plant if carefully grown, having attractive light and darker colouring running along the entire length of the slender, pointed leaves.

The main stem of the plant will need a supporting cane to remain upright. Plants sometimes produce young shoots naturally along the main stem so that multiheaded plants result. Alternatively, one can remove the growing tip of the main stem when the plant is about 60cm (2ft) tall, so that branching is encouraged. If plants are grown in soil that is constantly saturated, the incidence of leaf damage will be much increased. The soil for these plants should always be on the dry side, especially so during winter.

Feeding is not desperately important, but weak liquid fertilizer during the spring and summer months will do no harm; winter feeding is not advised.

Take care
Keep warm, light and dry. 66♦

Dracaena terminalis 'Firebrand'
(Flaming dragon tree)
● **Good light**
● **Temp: 18-24°C (65-75°F)**
● **Keep moist and fed**

Few foliage plants can match the rich red colouring of this dracaena though it is not the easiest of potted plants to care for. The colourful leaves are erect and spear-shaped.

Plants are grown by the nurseryman in a very open mixture composed mainly of pine leaf mould; this ensures that when water is poured onto the soil it drains freely through. It is preferable to use rain water, and to ensure that the soil is saturated each time. Avoid bone-dry conditions, but endeavour to allow some drying out of the soil between each soaking.

Good light is needed for *D. terminalis* to retain its bright colouring, but full sun through glass window-panes may cause scorching of foliage, so plants should be protected from such exposure. While new leaves are growing it will be important to feed plants at regular intervals, but it is not normally necessary to feed during the winter months.

Take care
Avoid excessive watering. 65♦

Eucalyptus gunnii
(Blue gum)
● **Good light**
● **Temp: 7-16°C (45-60°F)**
● **Keep moist and fed**

In the tropics the blue gums are invasive major trees, but for our purpose the smaller-leaved variety, *E. gunnii,* makes a very acceptable indoor plant, and is hardy outside in many areas. Rounded leaves have a grey-blue colouring that can be very pleasing in plant groupings.

For cooler areas that offer adequate light these are excellent plants that will overwinter without trouble if roots are not excessively wet while temperatures are at lower levels. During their more active summer months they will need regular watering and feeding. These are quite vigorous plants and should be regularly potted on during their early stages of growth. Peat-based potting mixes will be fine for plants in their early development, but as they advance beyond the 13cm (5in) pot it will be essential to use a loam-based potting mixture. Also, as plants tend to become tall and thin it is advisable to use clay pots, which will provide a more stable base than plastic ones.

Take care
Avoid wet winter conditions. 67♦

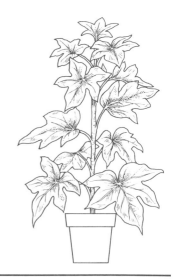

Euonymus japonicus medio-pictus
(Spindle tree)
- **Good light**
- **Temp: 7-18°C (45-65°F)**
- **Keep moist and fed**

This is another of the hardy outdoor plants that can be put to good use as subjects for indoor decoration. The leaves of this one are bright yellow in the centre with a green margin. With proper care it will grow to a height of 120cm (4ft). The woody stems can, however, be trimmed to a more manageable size at any time. There are other members of the euonymus family, such as the silver-foliaged *E. radicans*, which are more prostrate, and these will be the better for an annual clip into shape.

Good light is essential so plants need a fairly bright windowsill, but full sun will be harmful. Excessive watering will be damaging, particularly during the winter months when growth is less active. Feeding can be undertaken while plants are growing but should be discontinued in winter. When potting on a loam-based mixture is ideal.

Some branches will have a tendency to revert to green colouring, and it is best to cut these out.

Take care
Avoid hot, dry conditions. 69♦

Fatshedera lizei
(Ivy tree)
- **Light shade**
- **Temp: 4-16°C (40-60°F)**
- **Keep moist and fed**

This plant does not have the flexibility of the stems of *Hedera* (ivy), which is one of its parents, but is more in keeping with the stems of *Fatsia*, which is the other parent. Leaves have the shape of the ivy leaf and are glossy green in colour. For cooler locations the ivy tree is ideal, as it prefers low rather than high temperatures and is hardy in sheltered areas. Plants have a tendency to lose lower leaves, especially in hot, dry conditions.

New plants may be propagated either from the topmost section of the plant with three firm leaves attached or from sections of stem with a single leaf attached. In both cases they will do well in a temperature of around 18°C (65°F) if inserted in peat and sand mixture. In order to provide plants of full appearance, it is best to put three or four rooted cuttings in the growing pot rather than a single piece. The soil for potting up cuttings should be on the peaty side.

Take care
Avoid hot conditions. 68♦

Above: **Dracaena 'Firebrand'**
*This brilliantly coloured plant grows
to a height of 60-90cm (2-3ft) and*
*needs light and warm conditions.
Leaf discolouration may result from
wet soil through bad drainage.* 63♦

Above:
Dracaena marginata tricolor
The striking colours of the narrow leaves will develop well in good light. Soil should be kept on the dry side to prevent leaf drop. 62♦

Above: **Dracaena fragrans 'Massangeana'**
Strong, upright stems carry broad, gracefully curved leaves. 61♦

Below: **Eucalyptus gunnii**
An attractive blue gum with small leaves closely grouped on slender stems. Hardy in sheltered areas. 63♦

Above: **Euonymus japonicus**
Hardy out of doors, but also a fine bushy plant for cooler areas in the home. Good light will keep foliage colours really bright. 64♦

Left: **Fatshedera lizei**
The naturally glossy green leaves are attached to strong stems that should be supported so that the foliage can be seen to best advantage. 64♦

Below: **Fatshedera lizei variegata**
Yellow and white variegated forms are available, both of which need cool conditions to do well. 81♦

Left: **Ficus benjamina**
The elegant weeping fig has glossy green foliage and naturally cascading branches – a combination that produces one of the finest foliage plants. 81♦

Right: **Ficus benjamina 'Hawaii'**
Similar in appearance to the weeping fig, but of more erect habit and with brightly variegated leaves that are seen at their best in good light. 82♦

Below right: **Ficus lyrata**
Leaf shape gives the common name of fiddle leaf fig to one of the boldest and most vigorous indoor plants. Veined leaves are naturally glossy green. 83♦

Below: **Ficus europa**
Easily the best variegated form of broad-leaved rubber plants, with remarkably fine colouring and relatively easy to care for. 82♦

Left: **Ficus pumila**
Commonly named the creeping fig, it will also climb a damp wall or can be trained to a moss-covered support. The small, oval leaves are pale green and attached to wiry stems that have a natural twisting habit. 83♦

Right: **Fittonia argyroneura nana**
The silvery-grey colouring is heavily veined with a tracery of darker green that gives the oval leaves an attractive appearance. Plants have a creeping habit and need warmth and moisture. 84♦

Below: **Ficus robusta**
One of the symbols of the houseplant business, the rubber plant has broad glossy green leaves that are attached to stout upright stems. The leaves should be cleaned with a moist sponge. 84♦

Above: **Fittonia verschaffeltii**
Paper-thin leaves are of dull red colouring and are heavily veined, providing a plant of exotic appearance. Difficult to care for, the plant needs warm, moist, shady conditions. 85♦

Right: **Grevillea robusta**
When well grown the leaves of the silk oak have a silvery sheen that is most attractive. These vigorous plants need frequent feeding and cool, light conditions. 86♦

Below: **Gynura sarmentosa**
A member of the nettle family. The leaves are a vivid purple with a generous covering of tiny hairs that give the plant a rich glow of colour when seen in sunlight. 86♦

Above: **Hedera (small-leaved)**
*There are many shapes and colours
of these, all needing good light and
cool conditions. Plants will climb or
trail and all are hardy out of doors.*

Top left:
Hedera maculata
*With mottled greenish-gold foliage
this is one of the larger-leaved ivies.
It must have a supporting stake.* 88♦

Left:
Hedera canariensis
*In poor light the colourfully
variegated foliage will revert to
green. Offer good light.* 87♦

Right: **Hedera helix 'Goldchild'**
*Warm golden-yellow colouring
places this ivy ahead of most foliage
plants — it was once described as 'a
bowl of sunshine'.* 88♦

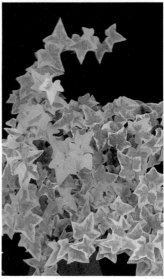

Above: **Helxine soleirolii**
*Minute bright green leaves are tightly
clustered and provide plants that are
neat hummocks of growth.* 89♦

Below: **Heptapleurum arboricola**
*Elegant, upright, green-foliaged
plants with palmate leaves that offer
a canopy of umbrella-like growth.* 89♦

Above: **Heptapleurum arboricola variegata**
Having the same habit as the green form but somewhat slower growing. The colouring is green and yellow with the latter predominating. 90♦

Above: **Hosta**
There are many attractive forms of these hardy plants, all developing into attractive clumps that need airy, light and moist conditions. 91♦

Below: **Hypoestes sanguinolenta**
The original spotted variety of this plant has been overtaken by a new one with much more pink. Needs light, moist conditions. 91♦

Fatshedera lizei variegata
(Variegated ivy tree)
- **Light shade**
- **Temp: 4-16°C (40-60°F)**
- **Keep moist and fed**

Most variegated plants are that little bit more difficult to care for than their green counterparts, and the variegated fatshedera is no exception. But provided it is not subjected to very high temperatures for long periods it will not prove too much of a problem.

Plants should be kept moist and well fed during the growing season and on the dry side with little or no feeding in winter. In agreeable conditions they will grow quite quickly on long single stems. However, the tip of the plant can be removed to encourage side shoots to grow and give the plant a more attractive appearance.

Besides the white variegated form there is now a cultivar with more golden foliage often labelled as *F. lizei aurea*. In my experience of growing the latter it would seem to be a marginally more difficult plant to care for, but none of the fatshederas can be classed as difficult.

Take care
Avoid hot and dry conditions. 69♦

Ficus benjamina
(Weeping fig)
- **Good light, no direct sun**
- **Temp: 16-21°C (60-70°F)**
- **Keep moist and fed**

Of very graceful weeping habit, *F. benjamina* will develop into tree size if provided with the right conditions. However, excess growth can be trimmed out at any time. To maintain plants in good condition with their glossy leaves gleaming it is important to feed them well while in active growth, and to pot them on into loam-based mixture as required. Little feeding and no potting should be done in winter, and it is also wise during this period to water more sparingly unless the plants are drying out in hot rooms. The weeping fig has a tendency to shed leaves in poorly lit situations.

Not many pests affect ficus plants, but scale insects seem to favour *F. benjamina.* These are either dark or light brown in colour and cling to stems and the undersides of leaves. Another sign of their presence will be dark sooty deposits on leaves below where the pests are clinging. It is best to wash them off with malathion.

Take care
Avoid placing in dark areas. 70♦

Ficus benjamina 'Hawaii'
(Variegated weeping fig)
- **Light shade**
- **Temp: 16-21°C (60-70°F)**
- **Keep moist and fed**

A recent introduction with white-and-green variegated leaves that seems likely to become a very successful indoor subject.

To get the best from these plants they need good light without bright sun, and the temperature should not fall below 16°C (60°F). Watering should follow the standard procedure for larger indoor plants, ie well watered from the top with surplus water clearly seen to drain out of the bottom of the container. The plant should then be left until the soil has dried out to a reasonable degree before watering again.

Younger plants should be provided with a supporting stake and the plant tied to the stake as new growth develops. However, a few strands should be allowed to hang over so that a plant with weeping growth all the way up results.

Like the green *F. benjamina*, this will tend to shed leaves at a rather alarming rate if it is placed in too dark a location.

Take care
Avoid placing in dark areas.71♦

Ficus europa
(Variegated rubber plant)
- **Good light**
- **Temp: 16-21°C (60-70°F)**
- **Keep moist and fed**

Far and away the best variegated broad-leaved rubber plant ever to be produced. Leaf colouring is a bright cream and green and the stems are bold and upright. Unlike previous variegated rubber plants this one does not have the usual tendency to develop brown discolouration along its leaf margins, and it is altogether more vigorous.

Taller plants will require supporting stakes, and ample watering and feeding while new leaves are being produced. This should be all year except during the winter months. However, some plants are slow to get on the move and such plants should be watered with care until it is seen that new leaves are on the way at the top of the stem.

All the broad-leaved rubber plants will be the better for cleaning with a damp cloth or sponge periodically, but one should not be too enthusiastic when it comes to use of chemical cleaners.

Take care
Avoid wet winter conditions.70♦

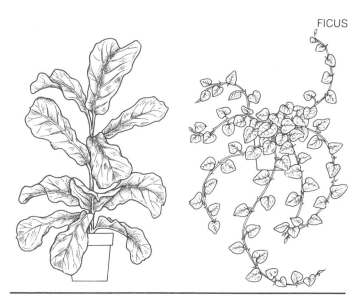

Ficus lyrata
(Fiddle leaf fig)
- **Light shade**
- **Temp: 16-21°C (60-70°F)**
- **Keep moist and fed**

One of the more majestic members of the fig family, *F. lyrata* develops into a small branching tree. Leaves are glossy green with prominent veins and, as the common name suggests, are shaped like the body of a violin. The original single stem of the plant will naturally shed lower leaves and the plant will produce leaf buds in the axils of the topmost four to six leaves, and in time these will become the branches of the tree.

It is important to seek out plants that have fresh, dark green leaves rather than those that may be marked or discoloured. Indoors they should be offered reasonable light and warmth, and in their early stages of development they will need careful watering; the plants are best kept on the dry side rather than too wet. More mature plants in larger pots will require more watering and more frequent feeding, with less of both being given in winter. The plant can be pruned at any time to improve its shape.

Take care
Avoid cold draughts. 71♦

Ficus pumila
(Creeping fig)
- **Light shade**
- **Temp: 16-21°C (60-70°F)**
- **Keep moist**

A simple plant, yet one of my personal favourites. Leaves are quite small as ficus plants go and are oval in shape. The plant may climb if provided with a support, or be allowed to trail in a natural manner. A good plant for mixed displays.

These plants must have reasonable temperature, and it is imperative that they be kept moist at all times; drying out of the soil will almost inevitably result in the loss of the plant. However, plants should not become sodden through standing permanently in water. They will tolerate drying out a little between waterings, but it must not be excessive. Feed them while they are growing, giving little or none in winter, and when potting on use a peaty mixture.

Cleaning individual leaves can be tedious, and I would suggest that a quick and adequate job can be done by inverting the plant in a bucket filled with soapy water and giving it a good swish around.

Take care
Avoid very dry conditions. 72♦

Ficus robusta
(Rubber plant)
- **Light shade**
- **Temp: 10-18°C (50-65°F)**
- **Avoid very wet conditions**

Almost the symbol of the modern-day houseplant business, the rubber plant is still grown and sold in large quantities. *Ficus robusta* now seems firmly established as the favourite rubber plant, and we seldom see its predecessors these days. The original variety was *F. elastica*, which in time was replaced by *F. decora*. The new plant is superior in almost every way, particularly in its ability to stand up to indoor conditions.

Failure with these plants usually arises from overwatering. Permanently wet soil results in roots rotting away, which will mean loss of leaves. It is especially important to prevent plants becoming too wet during the winter months. During the winter it is also wise to discontinue feeding. Potting should be undertaken during late spring or early summer, using loam-based mixture. Leaves will be brighter if occasionally cleaned with a damp sponge.

Take care
Protect from sun through glass. 72♦

Fittonia argyroneura nana
(Little snakeskin plant)
- **Shade**
- **Temp: 18-24°C (65-75°F)**
- **Keep moist and humid**

The smaller-leaved version of the silver snakeskin plant is much less demanding than its big brother. The leaves are oval in shape and produced in great quantity by healthy plants. Neat growth and prostrate habit makes them ideal for growing in bottle gardens or disused fish tanks.

Cuttings roots with little difficulty in warm, moist and shaded conditions. Several cuttings should go into small pots filled with peaty mixture, and it is often better to overwinter these small plants rather than try to persevere with larger plants. At all stages of potting on a peaty mixture will be essential, and it is better to use shallow containers that will suit the plant's prostrate growth.

Not much troubled by pests; the worst enemy by far is low temperature allied to wet root conditions. Recommended temperature levels must be maintained, and this is especially important during cold weather.

Take care
Avoid wet and cold combination. 73♦

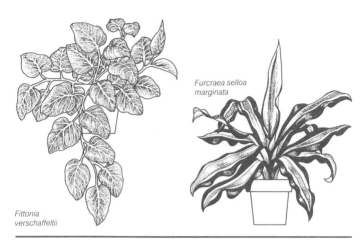

*Furcraea selloa
marginata*

*Fittonia
verschaffeltii*

Fittonia
(large-leaved)
(Snakeskin plant)
- **Shade**
- **Temp: 18-24°C (65-75°F)**
- **Keep moist and humid**

There are two of these that one will
be likely to come across, neither of
them very easy to care for. With large
reddish-green leaves there is *F.
verschaffeltii*, and with attractively
veined silver leaves there is *F.
argyroneura*. Both are of prostrate
habit, with leaves tending to curl
downwards over their containers. In
my experience these plants rarely do
well on the windowsill. They fare
much better in miniature
greenhouses, disused fish tanks or
bottle gardens. In such situations the
plants are free of draughts.

Bright sunlight will play havoc with
the tender foliage so these plants
must be in the shade, but not
necessarily in very dark locations.
When applying water it is best to
warm it slightly and to dampen the
area surrounding the pot as well as
the soil in which the plants are
growing. Frequent but small feeds
will be better than occasional heavy
doses – a little with each watering.

Take care
Avoid low temperatures. 74♦

Furcraea
- **Good light**
- **Temp: 13-21°C (55-70°F)**
- **Keep moist and fed**

There are several of these that one
may come across, and where
reasonable space can be offered
they can develop into spectacular
plants. The thick, fleshy leaves
radiate from the centre of the plant in
the form of a rosette and in some
varieties they may grow to a length of
120-150cm (4-5ft). For such
specimens adequate space is
essential, particularly as the larger
sorts have vicious-looking spines.

Growing these plants should not
be too much of a problem provided
they have a reasonable temperature
and are not allowed to become
excessively dry at their roots.
Feeding the more massive
specimens will have to be done with
some thoroughness and will mean
each time the plant is watered.

Besides the very large kinds there
is *F. foetida*, which produces leaves
45cm (18in) in length. But this one
will also present a few problems as
the spiny leaves are very stiff.

Take care
Be wary of the spined leaves.

Grevillea robusta
(Silk oak)
- **Light shade**
- **Temp: 4-21°C (40-70°F)**
- **Feed and water well**

An Australian plant, the silk oak makes a splendid tree in its native land, and is a fairly fast-growing pot plant in many other parts of the world. It is tough, has attractive, green silky foliage and is one of the easiest plants to care for. It can be readily raised from seed.

The grevillea will quickly grow into a large plant if it is kept moist and well fed, and if it is potted into a larger container when the existing one is well filled with roots. A loam-based soil is best. If plants become too tall for their allotted space it is no trouble to remove the more invasive branches with a pair of secateurs – almost any time of the year will do for this exercise.

During the summer months when the plant is in full vigour it will be important to ensure that it is obtaining sufficient water, and this will mean filling the top of the pot and ensuring that the surplus runs right through and out at the bottom drainage holes.

Take care
Water well in summer. 75♦

Gynura sarmentosa
(Velvet plant)
- **Good light**
- **Temp: 13-18°C (55-65°F)**
- **Keep moist and fed**

Scented flowers are a bonus with almost all plants, but the gynuras have been blessed with a scent that is obnoxious enough to be almost damaging to the senses. Weedy flowers appear in summer and should be removed before they have a chance to open. However, there are almost always compensations in nature and the gynuras are favoured with violet-tinged foliage that is hairy and very striking when seen in sunlight. They will grow at a rampant pace in light conditions if they are being watered carefully and fed regularly. Given a supporting cane plants can be encouraged to climb, but they are seen at their best when trailing from a pot or basket.

Untidy growth can be trimmed back at almost any time, and firm pieces may be used for propagating new plants. This should be done regularly as older plants tend to become untidy and lose their bright colouring. It is best to put several cuttings in each pot and to pinch out tips for bushy plants.

Take care
Replace older plants every year. 74♦

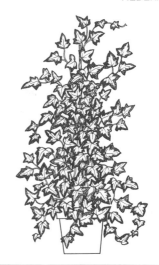

Hedera canariensis
(Canary Island ivy)
- **Good light**
- **Temp: 4-16°C (40-60°F)**
- **Keep moist and fed in summer**

This is one of the most rewarding indoor plants of them all, having bright green-and-white variegation and being reasonably undemanding to grow. The principal need is for light, cool conditions and a watering programme that allows for some drying out of the soil between each good soaking.

Plants can be encouraged to climb or trail, and they are excellent for those difficult cooler places such as hallways. In hot, dry conditions the plants are likely to become infested with red spider mite. These are minute insects that increase at an alarming rate if left to their own devices. In time the mites will make tiny webs from one part of the plant to another, but initially they are difficult to detect and are almost invariably found on the undersides of leaves. When infested with mite the leaves tend to curl inwards and appear hard and dry. Thorough and frequent drenching with insecticide is the best cure and should be done carefully out of doors on a still day.

Take care
Avoid hot, dry conditions. 76♦

Hedera Golden Heart
(Jubilee ivy)
- **Good light**
- **Temp: 4-16°C (40-60°F)**
- **Keep moist and fed in summer**

When well-grown there are few plants that can match the gold-and-green colouring of this small-leaved ivy. Large plants trained to a framework or growing against a wall can be especially pleasing. But the qualifying word here is 'well-grown', as these plants can often be thin single strands that do little for their surroundings. It is important to ensure that six, eight, or even 10 cuttings go into the propagating pot, so that the end result is a full and attractive plant. Pinching out the tips to induce a more bushy habit does not work with *H.* Golden Heart, which simply produces a single new shoot.

In good light the variegation will be improved, but bright sun should be avoided. In summer plants will have to be kept moist all the time and fed regularly, but in winter feeding should stop and much less water be given. During the summer months a sheltered spot out of doors will be much better than keeping plants inside, where the temperature may be too high.

Take care
Avoid wet winter conditions.

Hedera maculata

Hedera helix 'Goldchild'

(Golden English ivy)
- **Good light**
- **Temp: 7-16°C (45-60°F)**
- **Keep moist and fed**

One of the loveliest ivies of them all, having green-and-gold foliage with the latter being much the more predominant. Shallow plastic saucers for larger flower pots are excellent for displaying them in. Saucers should have holes made in their base, and several young plants are then planted in the containers. The result will be a flat mass of golden greenery that I once heard described as 'a bowl of sunshine'. When incorporating ivies in indoor displays, however, it is important to ensure that the position is not too hot and dry.

Cool, light conditions are best, and will help considerably in reducing the incidence of red spider mite. Smaller-leaved ivies develop a black rot among their stems and foliage if they are allowed to become too wet and the conditions are dank and airless. When watering, give a thorough application and then allow to dry reasonably before repeating. Feed in spring and summer.

Take care
Avoid hot and dry conditions. 77♦

Hedera (large-leaved)
- **Light shade**
- **Temp: 4-16°C (40-60°F)**
- **Keep moist and fed**

There are several larger-leaved ivies, other than *H. canariensis*, that are good for use as backing plants in arrangements either indoors or out.

Possibly the best-known of these is *H. maculata*, with dull gold and green mottled foliage, which makes a fine plant when trained to a support. With larger, very dark green leaves, each with a dull yellow splash in the centre, there is *H.* 'Goldleaf', one of the quickest growing of all the ivies. Also with very dark leaves, but unrelieved by other colouring, there is *H.* 'Ravenholst'. Perhaps the best of the larger-leaved forms, albeit seldom available, is *H. marmorata*, which has stiff, twisting stems and firm, well-variegated leaves.

As with almost all the other hederas, these plants will do better in cooler conditions, and should be well fed and watered during the more active summer months of the year. They will also attract red spider mites, which can be very harmful to the plant if allowed to go unchecked.

Take care
Avoid high temperatures. 76♦

Helxine soleirolii
(Mind your own business)
- **Light shade**
- **Temp: 4-18°C (40-65°F)**
- **Keep moist**

There are green- and golden-foliaged kinds, with the latter being the better choice. Although they will become straggly and untidy in time, the helxines are generally seen as neat mounds of minute leaves that make a pleasant change from the usual run of houseplants. Almost any pieces that may be snipped off when tidying up will make new plants if placed in peaty compost.

Shallow pans suit their low growth best and they will do well on almost any light windowsill. Plants should be watered carefully by pouring water into the pot under the leaves; water poured over the leaves will disarrange the neat mounds of growth and mar the plants' appearance. Less water is needed in winter, and no feeding, although a weak feed regularly given in summer will be appreciated.

A loam-based compost will be best when it comes to potting on, and regular trimming around with scissors will maintain a neat shape.

Take care
Periodically renew older plants.78♦

Heptapleurum arboricola
(Parasol plant)
- **Good light, no strong sun**
- **Temp: 16-21°C (60-70°F)**
- **Keep moist and fed**

In some parts of the world this plant may be seen labelled as *Schefflera*, which it strongly resembles. However, the difference lies in the size of the leaves. Both are green and palmate, but the schefflera leaf is very much larger.

Marginally more difficult to care for than *Schefflera* the parasol plant has an alarming habit of shedding leaves for no apparent reason. My view is that they often get much colder than the temperature recommended here. If plants are very wet at their roots and are subjected to low temperatures as well they will almost certainly lose leaves. There is some compensation, however, in that plants produce fresh growth later if the conditions improve.

Individual stems will grow to a height of 3m (10ft) in a comparatively short time. However, one can cut the stem back to more manageable size at any time of the year. As a result of this pruning treatment the plant will produce many more side growths.

Take care
Avoid winter wetness and cold. 78♦

Heptapleurum
'Geisha Girl'

Heptapleurum arboricola variegata
(Variegated parasol plant)
- **Good light, no strong sun**
- **Temp: 16-21°C (60-70°F)**
- **Keep moist and fed**

The fingered leaves and habit of growth are exactly the same as the green form, but the leaves are liberally splashed with vivid yellow colouring to give the plant a glowing brightness when it is placed among others in a large display. Elegance lies in the graceful and light distribution of leaves and stems, which enables one to see through and beyond to other plants in the display. And indoors it is equally important to have graceful plants rather than a solid wall of foliage.

In common with almost all the variegated plants this one should have a light location, but exposure to bright sun close to window-panes should be avoided if the leaves are not to be scorched. This is especially important if the leaves have been treated with chemicals. Most of the leaf-cleaning chemicals are perfectly suitable for the majority of plants, but one should never expose treated plants to direct sunlight.

Take care
Avoid winter wetness and cold. 79♦

Heptapleurum varieties
(Parasol plant)
- **Good light, no strong sun**
- **Temp: 16-21°C (60-70°F)**
- **Keep moist and fed**

One of the new green varieties is *Heptapleurum* 'Geisha Girl', which has more rounded leaves than the original and, when grown as a bushy plant with several pieces in the same pot, is in many ways superior.

Of dwarfer habit and with much smaller leaves there is *H. arboricola* 'Hong Kong', which has the added advantage of being easy to raise from seed. This one and all the others can be propagated from cuttings. These should consist of a piece of stem with a leaf attached and should be placed in small pots of moist peat in a temperature of not less than 21°C (70°F). Once rooted, all of the parasol plants will benefit from being potted on into slightly larger containers using loam-based potting mixture.

Active plants will require frequent watering and feeding during the summer months, but less water is required in winter and no feed should be given.

Take care
Avoid winter wetness and cold.

Hosta
(Plantain lily)
- **Light shade**
- **Temp: 4-21°C (40-70°F)**
- **Keep dry in winter, wet summer**

These are marginal houseplants, and have the added disadvantage that because they are deciduous they are often lost or forgotten during the winter months.

Despite these drawbacks I find them very useful as clumps in large tubs in cooler locations around the house, and we seem to be seeing new varieties all the time. All of them are superb when used as foliage accompaniment to flowers in mixed arrangements.

During the summer plants should be kept very moist and regularly fed. As they die down naturally in late summer only the minimum amount of moisture should be maintained in the soil until new growth is seen.

New plants are very easily made by dividing larger clumps in the autumn and planting them individually in pots. A peaty mixture with some loam added will suit them fine. Older plants can be planted successfully in the garden.

Take care
Avoid bright sun through glass. 80♦

Hypoestes sanguinolenta
(Freckle face; Polka dot plant)
- **Good light**
- **Temp: 10-16°C (50-60°F)**
- **Keep moist and fed**

In the last few years the hypoestes has enjoyed a new lease of life through the introduction of a much more colourful cultivar with a greater proportion of pink in its leaves.

Plants are easy to manage, although they frequently suffer through being confined to pots too small for the amount of growth that these quick growers will normally produce. Any purchased plant that appears to be in too small a pot should be potted into a larger one without delay. Use loam-based potting soil, as peat mixtures can be fatal for this plant if they dry out excessively. Also, it is wise to remove the growing tips so that plants branch and become more attractive. Untidy or overgrown stems can be removed at any time, and firm pieces about 10cm (4in) long can be used for propagation.

Extremely dry soil will cause loss of lower leaves, so check daily to ensure that the soil is moist.

Take care
Avoid drying out of soil. 80♦

91

Iresine herbstii
(Blood leaf)
- **Good light**
- **Temp: 13-18°C (55-65°F)**
- **Keep fed and watered**

These fall among the cheap and cheerful range of plants, and have foliage of a very deep, almost unnatural red. Cuttings root very easily and plants are quick to grow; they can be propagated successfully on the windowsill if shaded from direct sun.

Mature plants, however, must have a very light place if they are to retain their colouring, and will only need protection from strong midday sun. During the spring and summer plants must be kept active by regular feeding and ensuring that the soil does not dry out excessively. When potting on becomes necessary a loam-based mixture should be used; plants will soon use the nourishment in peat mixes even if fed regularly. At all stages of growth the appearance of the plant will be improved if the tips are periodically removed.

Besides the red-coloured variety there is *I. herbstii aureoreticulata*, which has yellow colouring and needs the same attention.

Take care
Feed well in summer.

Iris pallida
- **Good light**
- **Temp: 10-16°C (50-60°F)**
- **Keep on the dry side**

There are many hardy outdoor plants that are perfectly suitable as houseplants, and this is most assuredly one of them. In a pot it seldom grows more than 30cm (1ft) high, with overlapping fans of boldly striped green-and-white leaves.

Plants do best in shallow pans of loam-based potting mixture with plenty of drainage material in the bottom of the pan. If the soil is sluggish and slow to dry out the leaves will have a droopy, tired appearance; in a well-drained, dryish mixture the leaves will remain more attractively erect. Feeding is not desperately important, but very weak fertilizer given during the summer months will aid plants that have been in the same pots for a long time.

Propagation is simply a matter of removing plants from their pots, pulling the clumps of leaves apart and potting the divided pieces into small, shallow pots of their own.

Take care
Avoid excessive watering and feeding. 97♦

Kentia belmoreana
(Sentry palm)
- **Light shade**
- **Temp: 16-21°C (60-70°F)**
- **Water and feed well in summer**

This is also seen under its other name of *Howea belmoreana*. As a young plant it will be fine for indoor decoration, but as time goes on it will outgrow all but the largest of rooms. Growth can be contained to some degree in much the same way as trees are grown by the Bonzai method in Japan and elsewhere. The roots are hard pruned every second or third year causing the plant to become shorter and more stunted, with a bulbous base to its trunk. In one of my greenhouses I have two such plants that are almost 50 years old, yet they are only just over 3m (10ft) high.

Once these plants become old and well established they seem much easier to care for than in their early years. Mine are lightly shaded from the sun and are well watered during the summer months while they are producing their usual one or two leaves. They are kept on the dry side in winter.

Take care
Avoid wet winter conditions.97♦

Kentia forsteriana
(Paradise palm)
- **Light shade**
- **Temp: 16-21°C (60-70°F)**
- **Water and feed well in summer**

Kentia forsteriana is one of the most elegant and interesting of all the plants grown in pots for indoor decoration, but it is tending to become increasingly expensive. Also known as *Howea forsteriana* – most of the seed for growing these plants commercially still comes from their natural home of Lord Howe Island in the South Pacific.

To grow well all palms need an open, fibrous potting mixture, and it is wise to put a layer of clay pot shards in the bottom of the container.

The long upright leaves of these plants are sensitive to many of the chemicals used for controlling pests and for cleaning foliage, so it is wise to test any products on a small section of the plant before going in at the deep end and treating it all over. When testing such chemicals one should wait for at least a week to see what the reaction may be. It is also very unwise to expose plants to full sun or to cold conditions following any application of chemicals.

Take care
Avoid wet winter conditions.

Leea coccinea rubra
- **Light shade**
- **Temp: 16-21°C (60-70°F)**
- **Keep moist and fed**

This is a relative newcomer that may well become a very popular and trouble-free houseplant. It belongs to the Araceae family and is compact and neat, with numerous leaves closely set together on short stout stems. Leaves are open and finely cut, and are of rich russet colouring. The habit is not unlike that of its relative, *Aralia sieboldii*. Although the colouring of the foliage is a little better in good light the plant does not seem to object unduly to growing in more shaded locations.

As small plants they do well enough in peaty mixtures, but clearly approve of being potted into loam-based soils when going into 13cm (5in) pot sizes and larger. The pot should have plenty of drainage material placed in the bottom and the potting soil must be reasonably firm. Water well after potting and then keep the soil on the dry side until the plant has established in the new mixture. Once settled, plants should be fed each week when active.

Take care
Keep out of cold draughts. 98♦

Maranta erythrophylla
(Herringbone plant)
- **Light shade**
- **Temp: 18-24°C (65-75°F)**
- **Moist soil and atmosphere**

With reddish-brown colouring and intricately patterned, rounded leaves, this is one of our more attractive smaller plants. Exotic colouring immediately suggests that it is difficult, but the reverse is true if sufficient warmth is maintained and reasonable care given.

These plants are best grown naturally with foliage trailing where it will. Unless the leaves are misted twice daily, hanging containers will usually prove to be too dry a location for them; it will be better to grow plants at a lower level. To improve humidity around the plant place the pot in a larger container with moist peat packed between the two pots.

Peaty mixture is essential when potting on, but one should not be too hasty in transferring plants to very large pots. Fertilizer should be very weak and given with each watering rather than in a few heavy doses.

In time the plants will become ragged and it may then be wise to start again with new cuttings.

Take care
Avoid bright sunlight. 99♦

Maranta kerchoeviana
(Rabbit's tracks)
- **Shade**
- **Temp: 16-21°C (60-70°F)**
- **Moist soil and atmosphere**

Dark spots on grey-green leaves give this plant its unusual common name; the dark spots are said to resemble the tracks left by a rabbit. One of the older established houseplants, it is one of the easiest of this family to care for. It needs protection from direct sunlight and must be reasonably warm. Frequent feeding with weak liquid fertilizer is best, and one should use a peaty potting mixture.

When watering the soil should be moist but not totally saturated for very long periods, especially in winter. The danger with peat mixtures is that they will soak up very much more water than the plant is ever likely to need and will become totally waterlogged – a dangerous condition for most plants. For this reason plants should not be watered from the bottom and allowed to absorb water from the pot saucer. It is very much better to water into the top of the pot, giving sufficient to ensure that surplus drains away.

Take care
Avoid bright sunlight. 98♦

Monstera deliciosa
(Swiss cheese plant; Mexican breadfruit)
- **Light shade**
- **Temp: 16-21°C (60-70°F)**
- **Moist roots, regular feeding**

The naturally glossy green leaves with attractive deep serrations make the monsteras among the most popular of all indoor foliage plants. The aerial roots produced from the stems of more mature plants are an interesting and often perplexing feature. Removing some excess roots will not be harmful, but in most instances it is better to tie the roots neatly to the stem of the plant and to guide them into the pot soil.

As plants mature they will naturally produce serrated leaves, but darker growing conditions can result in leaves that are smaller and complete, rather than cut out. Bright sunlight magnified by window glass can cause scorching of foliage and should be avoided, particularly while soft new leaves are maturing.

Monsteras belong to the Araceae family and in their natural jungle environment will tend to scramble along the floor before finding a tree trunk to climb.

Take care
Avoid exposure to direct sunlight.100♦

Mimosa pudica
(Sensitive plant)
- **Light shade**
- **Temp: 16-21°C (60-70°F)**
- **Keep moist and fed**

These are attractive little plants with fern-like foliage, which are grown as annuals, fresh seed being sown each spring and old plants discarded at the end of the summer. The main attraction of this particular plant lies in its habit of collapsing completely during the day when the foliage is touched. In time the plant becomes erect again, but it is an eerie sight.

These plants are frequently offered for sale in very small pots that have little nutrient left in the soil. These should be potted into standard houseplant mixture as soon as possible. The result will be a much greener, more vigorous plant.

Actively growing plants should be kept moist and fed regularly. Freshly potted plants should be allowed to establish in new soil before being fed. A position in light shade is suggested, but plants will tolerate some sunlight if not too bright.

New plants may be raised from spring-sown seed, or from cuttings of older plants taken in the autumn.

Take care
Pot on to avoid starvation.

Musa
(Banana plant)
- **Light shade**
- **Temp: 18-24°C (65-75°F)**
- **Keep moist and fed**

Any exotic fruit that can be grown as a potted plant indoors will give the owner a great deal of pleasure and excite the interest of almost every visitor. The banana plant is no exception. There are many different cultivars and some are much too large for indoor decorating. *M. cavendishii*, with its narrower and shorter leaves, is one of the best where space is limited.

All of these plants will require ample watering and feeding. Newly purchased plants should be promptly transferred to slightly larger containers using loam-based potting soil. In time plants may produce banana fruits, but this is unusual indoors. What is more likely is that the main stem, on attaining about 2m (6ft) in height, will begin to deteriorate as new shoots appear at the base. When no longer attractive the main stem should be cut out and the smaller plants given a chance to develop, as they most certainly will.

Take care
Check for red spider under leaves.

Above: **Iris pallida**
An attractive miniature iris with pale green-and-white coloured foliage. The neat clumps of growth can be divided at any time to make additional plants. Cool conditions and dryish soil at the roots. 92◆

Right: **Kentia belmoreana**
Majestic palms that will attain a height of 3m (10ft) with roots confined to pots. Green, fingered leaves radiate from a stout central trunk that will in time develop a bulbous base and add much to the appearance of the plant. 93◆

Above: **Leea coccinea rubra**
*A fine, relatively new plant to the
houseplant range with reddish
foliage that is dense and compact.
Does well in light or shade.* 94♦

Right: **Maranta erythrophylla**
*With reddish-brown and green-
coloured leaves that are most
intricately marked, these are very
colourful foliage plants.* 94♦

Below: **Maranta kerchoeviana**
*With pale green, darkly spotted
leaves, this is among the easiest of
the marantas to care for. For best
results offer moist, shaded and warm
conditions.* 95♦

Above: **Monstera deliciosa**
Interesting leaves are perforated in older plants and are deeply cut along their margins. Strong aerial roots are produced from the main stem and are a natural part of its attraction. 95♦

Left: **Neanthe bella**
The compact parlour palm is ideal for limited space, and does well in most locations other than cold and wet. Chemicals may damage foliage, more so if exposed to strong sun. 113♦

Right:
Neoregelia carolinae tricolor
Spectacular plants of the bromeliad family with flat rosettes of leaves overlapping at their base to make a watertight urn for water. 113♦

Left: **Nephrolepis exaltata**
Bold ferns of which there are numerous versions, all with strong green fronds spraying out from the centre of the plant pot. Shade and warmth are needed. 114♦

Below left:
Nephthytis 'White Butterfly'
Free-growing plants of the Araceae family needing moisture and shade to do well. Will climb or trail. 115♦

Right: **Palisota elizabetha**
Forms bold clumps of pale green leaves with white midribs. The plants can be propagated by dividing clumps into smaller sections. 115♦

Below: **Pandanus baptiste**
Magnificent plants needing ample space. Leaves are bright yellow in colour with spined margins and a spined keel on their undersides. 116♦

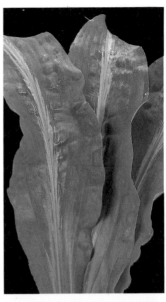

Above: **Pandanus veitchii**
This resembles a pineapple plant when young but becomes bolder with age. Leaves radiate from a short central trunk and are white and green variegated with spined margins and undersides. 116♦

Right: **Pellionia daveauana**
Naturally hanging or creeping plants that are easy to care for. Leaves are about 5cm (2in) in length and multicoloured. New plants can be propagated easily from cuttings. 117♦

Below: **Pellaea rotundifolia**
The button fern has very dark green, rounded leaves that form into densely foliaged plants in a comparatively short time. Shaded, moist and warm conditions. 117♦

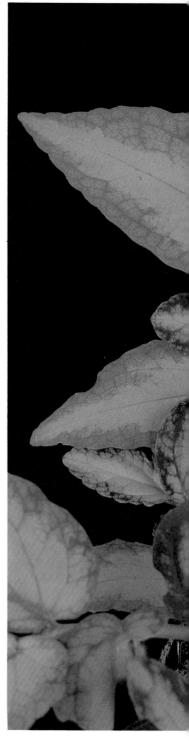

Above: **Peperomia argyreia**
With dark green markings on a silvery-grey background this is one of the most attractive of peperomias. Leaves have a natural shine. 118♦

Left: **Peperomia caperata**
The small leaves of this neat plant are produced in abundance and are a rich dark green in colour. A further attraction is their rough surface. 118♦

Right: **Peperomia hederaefolia**
Glossy, grey-coloured leaves are produced in quantity but remain small in size to form neat and compact plants that are in the easy-care category. 119♦

Above: **Peperomia magnoliaefolia**
Most popular of the peperomias, with glossy leaves that are brightly cream and green variegated. Leaves are fleshy and retain a lot of moisture, so reducing the need for watering. 119♦

Above:
Philodendron bipinnatifidum
Weedy plants when young but becoming most majestic with age. Keep moist. 120♦

Below: **Philodendron hastatum**
Glossy green leaves are broadly arrow-shaped. Plants attain stately proportions in time, but need supporting. 121♦

Above: **Philodendron scandens**
*The well-known sweetheart plant
has heart-shaped leaves that are
deep green in colour. Plants will
climb or trail.* 121♦

Right: **Phoenix roebelenii**
*When mature these palms are
among the most impressive of all
foliage plants, with fine leaves
radiating from a central stem.* 122♦

Below: **Phoenix canariensis**
*A tough tropical palm with coarse
foliage and a solid, gnarled trunk that
becomes a principal feature of the
plant as it ages.* 122♦

Above: **Pilea cadierei nana**
*Foliage of the aluminium plant is
generously speckled with silver.*

*Regular pinching out of the growing
tips will produce plants of neat
appearance. Easy to care for.* 123♦

Neanthe bella
(Parlour palm)
- **Light shade**
- **Temp: 16-21°C (60-70°F)**
- **Keep moist but well drained**

For people with limited space who wish to acquire a palm this is the answer, as the parlour palm presents a neat and compact plant throughout its life.

This plant is often used in bottle gardens, where it takes place of honour as the taller plant to give the miniature garden some height. One might add a word here to say that when planting bottle gardens it is most essential to ensure that small, non-invasive plants are selected.

The parlour palm should not be allowed to dry out excessively, although it should be a little on the dry side during the winter months, when growth is less active. It is important to ensure that the pot is well drained, and this will mean putting a layer of broken pieces of clay pot in the bottom of the new container before adding soil. Water poured onto the surface of the soil should be seen to flow fairly rapidly down through the mixture.

Take care
Avoid using chemicals on leaves.100♦

Neoregelia carolinae tricolor
(Blushing bromeliad; Cartwheel plant)
- **Good light**
- **Temp: 13-18°C (55-65°F)**
- **Dry at roots, urn filled**

Although it does produce small and inconspicuous flowers in the centre of the rosette of leaves (the 'urn' or 'vase') this is very much a foliage plant. Overlapping leaves radiate from a short central trunk and are spectacularly striped in cream and green with the added attraction, as flowers appear, of the shorter central leaves and the base of larger leaves turning a brilliant shade of red.

Following this colourful display the main rosette will naturally deteriorate and in time will have to be cut away from the small trunk to which it is attached. Take care that the small plant or plants forming around the base of the trunk are not damaged during this operation, as these will be the plants of the future. Leave the young plantlets attached to the stump to grow on or, in preference, remove them when they have developed several leaves of their own and pot them into peaty mixture.

Take care
Periodically change the water in the central urn of leaves. 101♦

Nephrolepis exaltata
(Ladder fern; Sword fern)
- ● Shade
- ● Temp: 16-21°C (60-70°F)
- ● Keep moist always

There are now many fine cultivars of this excellent plant. Any purchased plants that appear too large for their pots should be potted on without delay into a slightly larger container. A peaty mixture containing some loam will give better results than a soil that is thin and lifeless. As an alternative to putting the new plant into a conventional pot, transfer it to a decorative hanging basket.

Bright sunlight for any length of time will be fatal, as will excessive drying out of the soil. It will also be harmful should temperatures drop too low, if the soil in the pot is excessively wet. Plants will respond to feeding, but they often do better if fed with a foliar feed rather than a more conventional fertilizer taken up through the root system. New plants are normally raised from spores taken from the undersides of leaves when ripe, but may also be grown from the plantlets that develop on the runners of older plants.

Take care
Protect from direct sunlight. 102♦

Nephthytis 'Emerald Gem'
(Goose foot plant)
- ● Light shade
- ● Temp: 16-21°C (60-70°F)
- ● Keep moist

Also offered as *Syngonium podophyllum* 'Emerald Gem', this is one of the easiest of the aroid plants to care for indoors. In bright sunlight the plant will quickly deteriorate, but given moist, warm and shaded conditions it should be trouble-free.

It is an adaptable plant that may be grown as a trailing subject or encouraged to climb by offering some form of support. Being an aroid it will develop natural aerial roots along the main stem. It will assist the plant if the supporting stake can be covered with a layer of moss; the moss should be bound tightly to the support with non-corrosive plastic-covered wire, and kept moist. These plants also do well when grown by water culture. Although moisture at their roots and in the surrounding atmosphere is important, exercise care when watering, and ensure that the soil dries out a little between waterings, particularly during the winter. Feed regularly except in winter.

Take care
Keep moist, warm and shaded.

Nephthytis 'White Butterfly'

(Goose foot plant)
- **Light shade**
- **Temp: 16-21°C (60-70°F)**
- **Keep moist and fed**

Also known as *Syngonium podophyllum* 'White Butterfly'; the common name of goose foot relates to the shape of the adult leaf. Pale green leaves are suffused with white, and the plant will trail or climb as required.

It will have to be kept moist at all times, with occasional misting of the foliage with tepid water. The goose foot has adapted amazingly well to hydroculture, the technique of growing plants in water with nutrient solution added. In this instance the plant has all the soil washed away from its roots before it is converted to water culture. The roots are then suspended in clay granules (a sort of artificial pebble), and a special nutrient is added to the water for the plant to feed on. If the simple directions concerning watering and feeding are followed, the goose foot will grow at three times the rate of the same plant in soil, and frequent pruning is needed.

Take care
Avoid dry conditions. 102♦

Palisota elizabetha
- **Light shade**
- **Temp: 16-21°C (60-70°F)**
- **Keep moist and fed**

Years ago at the Chelsea Flower Show I noted large clumps of this in the exhibit of one of our botanical gardens. A chat with the man in charge made it possible for me to exchange with one of my plants. The lance-shaped dense leaves are produced from soil level and have a pale yellow central colouring with darker green outside. For show purposes it is an ideal plant that can be placed almost anywhere to good effect, and is especially useful for concealing the cumbersome pots of taller specimen plants. But it does not seem to appeal much to Mr. Average when he selects plants for the home; perhaps one day there will be a change of heart.

The plant is very easy to care for, but must be kept moist and fed. To make new plants the older clumps can be divided into smaller sections and potted into loam-based mixture at almost any time. Regular feeding of established plants will be important.

Take care
Never allow to dry out. Keep warm.103♦

Pandanus baptiste

(Screw pine)
- **Good light**
- **Temp: 16-21°C (60-70°F)**
- **Avoid too wet conditions**

This is probably the best-protected plant of them all. Vicious barbs are along the margins of the leaves, and a barbed keel runs the length of the underside of each leaf; all are capable of drawing blood if carelessly handled. However, it has the most incredible bright yellow colouring, which sets it apart from almost every other plant. The large recurving leaves are produced from a very stout trunk and will attain a length of 1.8m (6ft) and a width of 15cm (6in) or more when roots are confined to a pot. Should you be considering one of these for your home, be sure that you have a place large enough to accommodate it.

Older plants take on a further interesting dimension when they produce stout anchor roots from the main trunk; these extend in the manner of tent guy ropes around the plant to anchor it when hurricane winds hit its natural tropical island home. Maintain reasonable temperatures but treat them harshly to succeed.

Take care
Approach with caution! 103♦

Pandanus veitchii

(Screw pine)
- **Good light**
- **Temp: 16-21°C (60-70°F)**
- **Avoid too wet conditions**

Of the screw pines this is the most suitable for the average room, as it is reasonably compact and easier to accommodate. Leaves are green and white variegated and are produced in the shape of a large rosette, with leaves sprouting from a stout central stem. The screw pines all have vicious spines along the margins of their leaves, and a set of barbs running from the base to the tip of the leaf on the underside. Locate plants where they will be out of harm's way, perhaps by placing on a pedestal; this is also the best method of setting off these fine plants to advantage.

Being tough tropical plants that grow in exposed coastal areas, they are well adapted to harsh conditions. They will tolerate quite sunny locations and not be harmed provided they are not too close to the window-panes. Drought conditions seem to be taken in their stride, and they certainly prefer to be dry rather than too wet. Sharply draining, gritty soil is essential.

Take care
Handle plants with care. 104♦

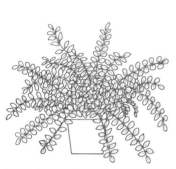

Pellaea rotundifolia
(Button fern)
- ● Shade
- ● Temp: 16-21°C (60-70°F)
- ● Keep moist

The button fern has dark green rounded leaves attached to firm, wiry stems, and forms a dense, attractive plant.

When potting use a peaty mixture and shallow pans. Almost all ferns in small pots will quickly become root bound and will lose their vigour if not potted on. However, inspection of roots can be misleading as these are very dark brown and the colour of the peaty soil in which they are growing, so careful inspection is needed before potting on.

Potting is best done in spring or summer and the new container should be only a little larger than the last. Roots ought to be moistened before it is removed from the pot, and after potting the soil should be well enough watered for surplus to be seen draining through the holes in the base of the pot. Then keep the newly potted plant on the dry side for several weeks — careful judgement is needed, as excessive drying out of the peaty mixture can be fatal as far as ferns are concerned.

Take care
Avoid direct sunlight. 104♦

Pellionia daveauana
- ● Light shade
- ● Temp: 13-21°C (55-70°F)
- ● Keep moist and fed

Very easy plants to care for, and easy to propagate, yet they never seem to make the grade as indoor plants. This is rather odd, as they adapt very well as hanging plants, or do well as a creeper, in the bottle garden, or simply as an addition to the windowsill collection. Leaves are oval-shaped and produced in quantity, and they have an interesting colouring of brown and dull yellow.

To propagate new plants, remove pieces of stem, any section, about 7.5cm (3in) long, and put four or five of these in small pots of peaty houseplant soil. Cuttings can go direct into hanging pots or small baskets if desired. When they get under way, remove the tips to encourage the plant to branch out. It is essential that plants be kept moist and warm, and out of direct sunlight. When potting on becomes necessary one of the many peaty houseplant potting mixtures will suit them fine, but avoid using very large pots.

Take care
Renew older plants periodically.105♦

Peperomia argyreia
(Rugby football plant)
- **Light shade**
- **Temp: 13-18°C (55-65°F)**
- **Keep moist and fed**

Sadly, this is one of the older houseplants that is not seen so frequently these days. The leaves are an interesting grey-green colour with darker stripes that radiate from the centre of the leaf. The darker stripes give the plant its name of Rugby football plant.

These compact plants should be grown in shallow pans of soilless potting mixture. The location must be light, with protection from direct sunlight. Watering should be done with care; err on the side of dry rather than wet conditions. Established plants can be given weak liquid fertilizer with every watering from early spring to late summer, but none in winter. Sound leaves can be removed and cut into quarters that are placed in upright position in pure peat in warm conditions. The quartered leaf will produce roots and eventually leaves along the length of the cut edge below soil level. During propagation, ensure that the cuttings do not become too wet.

Take care
Avoid winter wetness and cold. 106♦

Peperomia caperata
(Little fantasy)
- **Light shade**
- **Temp: 16-21°C (60-70°F)**
- **Never overwater**

This plant is neat and compact and ideally suited to growing on the windowsill, where it will not become entangled with curtains. Leaves are a blackish green in colour, and have an undulating surface. The rounded leaves are attached to long stalks that sprout directly from soil level.

Cuttings made by inserting individual leaves in peaty mixture will root with little trouble if a temperature in excess of 18°C (65°F) can be maintained. Rooted leaves produce clusters of small plants that should be potted into peaty houseplant soil when large enough to handle. Small pots should be used initially and plants ought to be gradually potted on from one size container to the next. Also, when potting low-growing plants of this kind, it is important not to select pots of full depth; shallower pans (or half pots) are now freely available. After potting, the soil should be kept on the dry side and plants should not be fed for at least three months.

Take care
Avoid placing in dark corners.106♦

Peperomia hederaefolia

(Silver ripple)
- **Light shade**
- **Temp: 16-21°C (60-70°F)**
- **Keep moist and fed**

Unusual glossy grey colouring sets *P. hederaefolia* apart from most other indoor plants. Stalked leaves are rounded in shape and emerge from soil level, there being no stem to speak of. At one time a great favourite in the houseplant league it now seems to have waned a little, probably resulting from other more interesting plants coming along to take its place. One of its main benefits lies in the fact that it occupies little space and is ideal for including in small planted arrangements of plants. Carboys are the typical example of close grouping that requires small plants that are not too invasive. Vigorous plants will quickly invade the growing space of every plant in the container.

This peperomia will enjoy a watering routine that allows the soil to dry out, but not bone dry, between each watering. It will also respond well to frequent weak feeds, but needs no feeding and less water in winter.

Take care
Avoid wet and cold combination. 107♦

Peperomia magnoliaefolia

(Desert privet)
- **Good light**
- **Temp: 16-21°C (60-70°F)**
- **Keep on dry side**

The common name and the thick fleshy leaves give some clues regarding the care of this neat and colourful little plant. The succulent fleshy leaves indicate that they are capable of holding a considerable amount of water, to withstand arid conditions.

The quickest way of killing desert privet is to keep it in poor light and on the cold side, and to have the soil very wet. One of the most important requirements will be to ensure that the soil dries out between each watering. Stem rot followed in all probability by the fungus disease botrytis will be the inevitable result of keeping plants too wet for too long.

Feeding is not important, but will have to be done occasionally – preferably not in winter and never in heavy doses. But in respect of nutrition there is one very important need, and that is, when potting plants on into larger containers, to use soilless potting mixture; anything else would be fatal.

Take care
Keep warm, light and dry. 108♦

Persea gratissima
(Avocado pear)
- **Good light**
- **Temp: 16-21°C (60-70°F)**
- **Keep moist and fed**

The foliage is green, coarse, and not particularly attractive, but there is the fascination of growing plants from the central stone of the fruit and no doubt a sense of achievement exists that encourages one to hang on to the plant. Very often they are left to become tall and ungainly when it would be better to pinch out the early growing tips of the plant to encourage it to branch out and adopt a better shape. Plants will also be thin and poor in appearance if they are allowed to languish in dark corners: good light is needed, but offer some protection from direct sunlight.

Raising plants from stones is relatively easy. Four cocktail sticks are pushed into the stone evenly spaced, and the stone is then suspended in a tumbler with the base submerged in about 5cm (2in) of water; in time the base of the stone will soften and roots will form in the water. When lots of roots are present the stone is potted in peaty soil.

Take care
Feed while actively growing.

Philodendron bipinnatifidum
(Tree philodendron)
- **Shade**
- **Temp: 16-21°C (60-70°F)**
- **Keep wet and fed**

There are numerous philodendrons of similar type to this one, all requiring ample space for their radiating leaves once they reach maturity. Because of their habit of growth these are essentially individual plants to be placed on their own rather than as part of a collection. Leaves are glossy green in colour and deeply cut along their margins, and held on stout petioles attached to very solid short trunks. In time aerial roots will be produced from the trunk; direct these into the pot soil when they are long enough. With older plants it may be necessary to remove some of these aerial roots, or they can be allowed to trail into a dish of water placed alongside.

Ample watering is a must, with marginally less being given in winter; and feeding should not be neglected. When potting on use a mixture containing some loam, as these are quite greedy plants. Most of them are raised from seed and young plants are usually available.

Take care
These plants need space. 109♦

Philodendron hastatum
(Elephant's ear)
- **Shade**
- **Temp: 16-21°C (60-70°F)**
- **Keep moist and fed**

Again we have a touch of majesty from the splendid Araceae family of plants, and the common name immediately gives the game away that this is a rather large plant. The leaves are broadly arrow-shaped, glossy green and attached to very bold, tall-growing stems; in a greenhouse it may reach a height of 6m (20ft). Normally indoor growth is thinner and less robust, but the fact that the plant has a tough constitution makes it a reasonably trouble-free plant in agreeable conditions.

As a young plant it will trail, but it is much too important for this style of growing and when purchasing one you should also acquire a moss-covered support (preferably one that can be extended) to which the plant can be tied. If the moss is kept moist by regular spraying with water from a mister it will be found that in time the natural aerial roots of the plant will grow around and into the moss. Leaves can be occasionally wiped with a damp cloth to clean them.

Take care
Avoid dry and sunny positions. 109◆

Philodendron scandens
(Sweetheart plant)
- **Shade**
- **Temp: 16-21°C (60-70°F)**
- **Keep moist and fed**

One of the smallest-leaved of all the philodendrons and possibly the best suited to the relatively smaller rooms of today. The leaves are heart-shaped and glossy green, and it may be encouraged to either climb or trail.

Keeping the soil moist, not saturated, is important, and occasional weak feeding will suit it well. Young plants should be potted into soilless potting mixture, but older plants will respond better if potted into a mix that contains a small proportion of loam. In ideal conditions plants may be potted at almost any time, but in the average home they will do much better if the potting can be done at the start of the summer. I am often asked for plant suggestions for dark corners and the questioner invariably wants something colourful. But such plants are few and far between; it is better to select green foliage for difficult spots, and the sweetheart plant is ideal in most cases.

Take care
Avoid dry and sunny places. 110◆

Phoenix canariensis
(Feather palm)
- ● **Good light**
- ● **Temp: 16-21°C (60-70°F)**
- ● **Keep moist**

In their tropical habitat these stately palms will grow to 9-12m (30-40ft) in height, but they are less vigorous when their roots are confined to pots. Leaves are coarse and open, and attached to short, stout trunks. Leaves have short petioles armed with vicious short spines, which make it necessary to handle the plant with care. Older plants are normally beyond the purse of the average person, so seek out plants of more modest size when shopping.

Smaller plants can be potted on into loam-based potting soil. Good drainage is essential, so broken flower pots or some other form of drainage material ought to be placed in the bottom of the pot before any soil is introduced. Well-drained soil is needed, but regular and thorough watering will be of the utmost importance while plants are actively growing. During growth, feed plants at regular intervals using a proprietary fertilizer and following the maker's directions.

Take care
Check occasionally for red spider. 110♦

Phoenix roebelinii
(Feather palm)
- ● **Good light**
- ● **Temp: 16-21°C (60-70°F)**
- ● **Keep moist**

Not unlike *P. canariensis* as a young plant, but later more feathery and delicate and less coarse in appearance. It is also less robust, retains its shape better, and will attain a height of around 1.5m (5ft) when grown.

Select loam-based potting mixture with some body to it. Good drainage will ensure that the soil in the pot will remain fresh and well aerated, which is essential if palm roots are not to rot and die. During the summer, plants can go out of doors in a sheltered, sunny location.

Not many pests bother this plant, but the ubiquitous red spider will usually be lurking around if the growing conditions tend to be very hot and dry. One should suspect their presence if plants become harder in appearance and develop paler colouring than usual. Some insecticides are harmful to palm plants, therefore it is wise to check suitability with your supplier before purchasing.

Take care
Ensure soil is well drained. 111♦

Pilea cadierei nana
(Aluminium plant)
- **Light shade**
- **Temp: 16-21°C (60-70°F)**
- **Keep moist and fed**

With silvered foliage, this is by far the most popular of the pileas, but there are numerous others, all needing similar treatment.

Plants are started from cuttings taken at any time of the year if temperatures of around 18°C (65°F) and moist, close conditions can be provided. A simple propagating case on the windowsill can offer just these conditions. Top cuttings with four to six leaves are taken, the bottom pair is removed and the end of the stem is treated with rooting powder before up to seven cuttings are inserted in each small pot filled with a peaty mixture. Once cuttings have got under way the growing tips are removed and the plants are potted on into slightly larger containers in loam-based mixture.

Plants should have ample light, but not be exposed to bright sunlight. Although small, pileas need ample feeding during the growing months, if they are to retain their bright colouring.

Take care
Pinch out tips to retain shape. 112♦

Pilea involucrata (P. spruceana)
(Friendship plant)
- **Light shade**
- **Temp: 16-21°C (60-70°F)**
- **Keep moist and fed**

The friendship plant has reddish-brown colouring, and is easy to propagate; it may have acquired its common name as a result of surplus plants being distributed around the neighbourhood.

Several other pileas may be propagated with equal ease, and one or two of them will further oblige by producing an abundance of seed that will pop about in all directions when ripe, with the result that all the other pots surrounding the seeding pilea will provide a welcome bed of moist soil for the seed to germinate in. It will be wise to treat these as weeds and remove them before they take over the living room.

The friendship plant provides a neatly rounded, low-growing plant with an unusual colouring. It keeps its neat appearance for perhaps two years indoors and then begins to develop longer and more straggly stems, which spoil the plants' appearance; it could then be wise to start again with fresh cuttings.

Take care
Keep it out of bright sunlight. 129♦

Piper ornatum
(Ornamental pepper)
● **Good light**
● **Temp: 18-24°C (65-75°F)**
● **Keep moist**

The waxy leaves are 7.5-10cm (3-4in) long, deep green in colour and beautifully marked in silvery pink. Provide plants with a light framework onto which they can be trained so that they are seen to full effect.

Warmth is essential, and the air around the plant must not become too dry; spray leaves with tepid water from a hand mister. When potting on, avoid large pots; these plants prefer pots in proportion to the top growth. Soilless potting mixture suits them best, but it will be important to ensure that the plant is fed regularly (not in winter) and that soil never becomes too dry. Very wet conditions will be equally harmful, so allow some drying out between waterings. Plants lose much of their colouring if grown in dark corners. Provide good light but avoid direct sunlight.

Firm leaves with a piece of stem attached can be rooted in peat in warm conditions during spring in a propagating case.

Take care
Avoid winter cold and wetness.

Pisonia brunoniana variegata
● **Light shade**
● **Temp: 16-21°C (60-70°F)**
● **Keep moist and fed**

These small tropical trees are useful plants with leaves about 30cm (12in) long, closely grouped on firm, upright stems. They have a neat habit of growth and attractively variegated leaves.

Good light with some protection from direct sunlight is necessary if plants are to retain their colourful variegation. To keep them in good fettle a reasonable, stable temperature is also needed. During the growing months plants require much more water than in winter, when care will be needed to ensure that the soil is never excessively wet; wet conditions at this time will cause roots to rot, with consequent loss of the lower leaves. Feeding is not necessary in winter, but should not be neglected for active plants.

New plants can be made from stem sections with one or two leaves attached, taken in spring; put them into small pots of peat, and place in a heated propagator. Use loam-based soil for growing on.

Take care
Avoid wetness and cold in winter.

Pittosporum eugenioides
(Parchment bark)
- **Good light**
- **Temp: 13-21°C (55-70°F)**
- **Keep moist and fed**

In the course of my duties it is almost inevitable that I should have favourite plants. For at least 20 years I have supervised the care of a pair of *P. eugenioides* plants that are now in the region of 3m (10ft) high and of full and attractive appearance. The pots in which they are growing are little more than 38cm (15in) in diameter – much too small, in the opinion of most plant growers, but my plants are superb and are sustained solely on regular feeding throughout the year, with the exception of the winter months. These plants seem to prove conclusively that plant pots of enormous size are not really necessary if the culture is correct.

The colouring of the leaves, which have attractively waved margins, is predominantly grey with a little white relief, and leaves are attached to firm, wiry stems. Good light is necessary and one must avoid excessive watering in winter to prevent browning of leaf margins.

Take care
Avoid dark locations. 130♦

Pittosporum garnettii
(Parchment bark)
- **Good light**
- **Temp: 7-16°C (45-60°F)**
- **Keep moist and fed**

A little-known plant, but very hardy both indoors and in the garden. The leaves are oval in shape, slightly wavy at their margins, and with a speckled grey-white silvery sheen to them. Against the light-coloured foliage the black stems provide a splendid contrast. In the garden over a period of about six years, young plants grow to a height of around 120cm (4ft), with a diameter of about 75cm (2ft 6in). Plants growing in pots and about the same age are roughly half the size.

Good light is essential if plants are to retain their colouring – and their leaves. Cool conditions will be more acceptable than high temperatures. Plants are better standing in large saucers than in decorative outer pots, which tend to accumulate unnoticed surplus, causing the soil to become waterlogged. With saucers one can see surplus water accumulate and tip it away.

Take care
Avoid dark areas and wet conditions.

Pittosporum tenuifolium
(Parchment bark)
- **Good light**
- **Temp: 7-18°C (45-65°F)**
- **Keep moist and fed**

This is much used for flower arrangements by florists. Bright green leaves have wavy margins, and the black stems provide an interesting contrast. They are quite colourful, develop a neat, bushy shape, and will tolerate cooler conditions and enjoy them rather than object by shedding leaves.

Start off small plants in peaty mixture, but from the 13cm (5in) size pot and upwards a loam-based mixture will be better. As these plants like fresh air and sunshine, pot them into decorative patio planters rather than the more conventional flower pot, and put them out of doors in summer.

On taking them in again it is fatal to place them immediately in darker areas; have them as near to a natural light source as possible where the conditions will be cool and airy.

Trimming off pieces of the plant for flower arrangements will be beneficial provided one is not too severe. Trimmed plants become bushier.

Take care
Keep in good light. 129▶

Platycerium alcicorne
(Stag's horn fern)
- **Shade**
- **Temp: 16-21°C (60-70°F)**
- **Keep moist**

Essential requirements of all platyceriums are moist, warm and shaded conditions, and if one cannot offer all three of those then it will be difficult to grow these plants.

Plants are normally grown in pots filled with peat mixture and will seldom do well in anything that is too heavy and root-restricting. But besides the conventional pot they may be grown as mobiles, or for hanging on a wall. The plant is removed from its pot and the roots are wrapped in fresh sphagnum moss before the complete bundle is firmly secured to its support: plastic-covered wire is useful for this purpose. The plant can then be soaked thoroughly in a bucket of water and allowed to drain before it is put in position. Subsequent watering should follow the same lines.

Scale insects attaching themselves to all parts of the plant are by far the worst pest, and should be wiped off with a firm sponge that has been soaked in insecticide.

Take care
Avoid excessive drying out. 130▶

Pleomele reflexa variegata
(Song of India)
- **Good light**
- **Temp: 16-21°C (60-70°F)**
- **Keep on dry side**

These painfully slow-growing plants are not often available: anyone seeing a priced plant should stake a claim immediately! When mature and well grown, this is a fine plant. Stems are very woody, and leaves are miniature but bright yellow. Plants may be no more than 1.5-1.8m (5-6ft) tall, though at least 20 years old. Slow growth is one reason for their scarcity, and for the high price should any be on offer.

Plants enjoy good light, with shade from strong sunlight, and temperatures that fluctuate from 16 to 21°C (60 to 70°F). Water well when necessary, and allow to dry appreciably before watering again, but the surrounding area should be kept moist at all times. Feeding should be done on average once a week in summer, with none at all from the onset of winter to the early spring when new growth appears.

Few pests bother these fine plants, whose worst enemy is a combination of wetness and cold.

Take care
Ensure soil drains freely. 131♦

Podocarpus macrophyllus
(Buddhist pine)
- **Light shade**
- **Temp: 10-16°C (50-60°F)**
- **Keep moist, less in winter**

The open foliage of this small tropical tree provides a pleasing potful of greenery for cooler locations indoors. If grown on a single stem it may attain a height of about 1.5m (5ft); but remove the growing tip when the plant is young, and it will become more bushy.

It abhors overwatering, which can be particularly damaging during winter. Avoid the practice of placing plants in a saucer and filling it with water. With modern peaty potting mixtures there will be much more water taken into the peat by capillary action than the plant is ever likely to need, so leading to root rot. Instead, fill the space between the rim of the pot and the soil each time the plant is watered. When watering from the top, one should see the surplus draining through the holes in the bottom of the container. Before watering again, allow the soil to dry.

When growing podocarpus plants indoors they do much better in cool, light conditions, and abhor heat.

Take care
No winter feeding required.132♦

Polyscias balfouriana
(Dinner plate aralia)
- **Light shade**
- **Temp: 16-21°C (60-70°F)**
- **Keep moist and fed**

This is another painfully slow grower that will take at least 10 years to reach 3m (10ft) in height, but in limited space this could be an advantage. Stems are woody and the leaf colouring is variegated white and green. Growth is very erect and plants seldom need to be staked. As the plant ages and increases in height, the lower stem will have a natural tendency to shed leaves.

Red spider mites seem to find this plant particularly appetizing. Although minute in size, these pests can increase at an alarming rate and completely blanket the plant to such an extent that it may well not recover. The layman often finds it difficult to believe that such minute pests can be so destructive. When they are detected, take action right away, by preparing a recommended insecticide solution and thoroughly saturating the undersides of all foliage. This task ought to be done out of doors on a warm day, and rubber gloves and a mask worn.

Take care
Check for pests under leaves. 133♦

Pteris cretica albo-lineata
(Variegated table fern)
- **Shade**
- **Temp: 16-21°C (60-70°F)**
- **Keep moist**

The variegated form of *P. cretica* has a pale green outer margin to its leaves and a cream-coloured central area. There are several other variegated forms available, and all will respond well to shaded and warm conditions where a reasonable degree of humidity can be maintained. They will also benefit from regular feeding once they have become established in their pots. Many of these smaller ferns do very well if fed with a foliar feed, which is sprayed onto the leaves.

Fern plants do very much better if they can be grouped together. Large plastic trays are easily obtainable, and these are ideal for placing groups of ferns and other types of indoor plants. The tray is filled with gravel and well watered before the plants are placed on the surface; it is important that the plant pot base should not stand in water, as this would make the soil much too wet. The wet tray will provide a continual source of essential humidity.

Take care
Never subject ferns to direct sun. 132♦

Above: **Pilea involucrata**
Sometimes known as the friendship plant because its ease of propagation makes its distribution among friends a simple matter. Neat hummocks of growth result if the leading growing tips are removed when they appear to be overgrowing. Frequent feeding is an essential need, and warm, light conditions will be a benefit. 123♦

Right: **Pittosporum tenuifolium 'Irene Patterson'**
One of the many improved forms of the New Zealand pittosporums. Glossy, evergreen foliage springs from woody stems and provides attractive plants in pots where the temperature is on the cool side and good light is available. Can be planted out of doors but is not altogether hardy, so needs protection from severe weather. 126♦

Above: **Pittosporum eugenioides**
*With grey-and-white variegated
foliage, these are essentially pot
plants for the cooler location indoors.
Good light is a further important
need. Stems are woody and leaves
have wavy margins.* 125♦

Right: **Pleomele reflexa variegata**
*Commonly named song of India, this
is an aristocrat among potted plants.
Foliage is almost entirely bright
yellow, with narrow leaves about
15cm (6in) long.* 127♦

Below: **Platycerium alcicorne**
*The foliage has a bluish-coloured
bloom that adds much to the
appearance of this fern. Anchor
fronds are intended to hold the plant
in position, while main fronds
resemble stags' antlers.* 126♦

Left: **Podocarpus macrophylla**
*Mature trees in their native habitat,
these plants have numerous,
narrow, evergreen leaves and make
fine bushy plants for cool places.* 127♦

Right:
Polyscias balfouriana 'Pinnochio'
*Leaves are rounded with pale cream
and green variegation. Stems are
woody and the plant is generally slow
growing. It needs careful culture if
the leaves are not to be shed
prematurely. Red spider mites are
troublesome.* 128♦

Below: **Pteris cretica albo-lineata**
*An attractive fern with pale green and
off-white variegation, and one of the
easiest ferns to care for. Needs
moist and warm shaded conditions
to thrive. Bright sun and dry air
conditions cause leaf scorch.* 128♦

Left:
Sansevieria trifasciata Laurentii
*The true type has bright yellow
margins to the leaves with mottled
variegation in the central areas.
These plants tolerate direct sunlight
and can be very durable if not
overwatered.* 147♦

Right: **Saxifraga sarmentosa**
*Aptly named the mother of
thousands because of the many
perfectly developed plantlets that
hang naturally from the parent plant,
this is essentially a trailing subject.
Propagation is a simple matter of
rooting plantlets.* 148♦

Below: **Schefflera digitata**
*With large-fingered leaves that are
attached to stout petioles, this is one
of the finest indoor green plants. The
leaves are naturally glossy green and
are attached to a strong central stem
that needs no form of support.* 148♦

Above:
Scindapsus 'Marble Queen'
One of the more difficult indoor plants. White dominates. 150♦

Top left: **Schefflera venusta**
A comparative newcomer, with narrow, palmate, undulating leaves. Colouring is a rich glistening green and the plant is of upright habit. 149♦

Left: **Scindapsus aureus**
Perhaps the best of all the foliage plants, with yellow and green variegation that is retained even in poor light. Will climb or trail. 149♦

Right: **Sedum morganianum**
A naturally trailing succulent plant with bluish-grey leaves that hang perpendicularly from the growing pot, which must be suspended. 150♦

Above: **Setcreasea purpurea**
*A member of the tradescantia tribe.
The leaves of this plant are purple all
over and attached to firm succulent
stems. The colour develops most
effectively when the plants are in
good light.* 152♦

Left: **Sparmannia africana**
*Large, pale green leaves of coarse
texture branch freely from stout
stems with many branches. It will in
time attain a height of about 2.4m
(8ft). An easy-care plant.* 153♦

Right: **Stenotaphrum secundatum**
*Amazingly vigorous plants that will
quickly fill their allotted space. They
can be used effectively in hanging
baskets. Leaves are narrow with
cream and green variegation.* 153♦

Above: **Tetrastigma voinierianum**
*A rampant member of the vine family
and perfect for covering an interior
wall with its invasive, pale green
growth and leaves. Natural tendrils
will cling to any support.* 154♦

Left: **Stromanthe amabilis**
*Similar in appearance to some of the
marantas, these plants form neat low
mounds of growth but need careful
culture to succeed. Warm conditions
suit them best.* 154♦

Below: **Tolmiea menziesii**
*The most endearing feature of this
plant is the way in which perfectly
shaped young plants form on the
stalks of parent leaves. Needs cool
conditions.* 155♦

Above: **Tradescantia 'Quicksilver'**
*Fine, easy-care plants with bright
silver variegation. Best in hanging
baskets.* 157♦

Below: **Vriesea mosaica**
*A rare member of the bromeliad
family with mainly reddish-brown
colouring.* 157♦

Above: **Yucca aloefolia**
*Stately plants for difficult locations, as they are very durable if not overwatered. These plants are normally seen as stout stems with tufts of growth at the top.*158♦

Above: **Zebrina pendula**
From the lowly tradescantia tribe, but a surprisingly colourful plant when

seen as a well-grown specimen in a hanging basket. The foliage of better plants has a silvery sheen. 158♦

Rhoeo discolor
(Moses in the cradle)
- **Shade**
- **Temp: 16-21°C (60-70°F)**
- **Keep fed and watered**

Related to the tradescantias, *R. discolor* is not a particularly attractive or exciting plant to have around, but it is interesting. Besides the common name above, there are several others, such as three men in a boat or Moses on a raft, all of them relating to the white flowers that nestle in a boat-like bract which develops at the base of the leaves. The leaves are green on their upper surface, striped with cream in the variegated form, and deep purple on the reverse of the leaf.

It will produce flowering bracts in time and these scatter seed in and around the pot, making propagation simple. This is a good thing, as plants tend to lose their attraction with age, and are better replaced periodically. A reasonable temperature is essential, and plants will do best in a lightly shaded location; they should be kept fairly moist at all times. Feeding need be undertaken only when growth is active. Potting soil should contain some loam.

Take care
Replace plants every second year.

Rhoicissus rhomboidea
(Grape ivy)
- **Light shade**
- **Temp: 13-18°C (55-65°F)**
- **Keep moist and fed**

Grape ivy is a tough old plant that seems to outlast all others. The three-lobed leaves are a bright glossy green. The plant should be offered some form of support through which it can entwine itself; but although generally considered to be a climber it will also do very well in a hanging container.

Plants are started from cuttings taken at any time if moist and warm conditions can be provided. When cuttings are potted put five or six into a small pot of peaty mixture.

Although tough enough to withstand harsh treatment they will fare better if kept moist and fed regularly in a location that offers reasonable light but not full sun. In bright sunlight, or if plants are starved, they become pale brown, and leaves will be generally smaller. Plants that have taken on a harder appearance may be in need of potting on, so root condition should be checked and plants potted if need be in loam-based mixture.

Take care
Avoid strong sunlight.

Rhoicissus rhomboidea 'Ellendanica'
(Grape ivy)
- Light shade
- Temp: 13-21°C (55-70°F)
- Keep moist and fed

The tri-lobed glossy foliage of *R. rhomboidea* should be familiar to everyone associated with indoor plants, but we now have from Denmark a plant with lightly waved leaf margins that add much to its attraction. The glossy foliage in well-grown plants has a burnished tinge.

It can withstand harsh conditions and survive happily. Of natural climbing habit, it will not take too unkindly to darkish locations indoors, but will obviously fare better in reasonable light, not direct sun. Keep plants moist and fed in spring and summer.

Pests are not a great problem, but mealy bug can sometimes cause difficulties. These bugs are easily seen, as small groups that resemble cotton wool, inside which the young bugs are protected. Mature bugs, with a white mealy appearance, will be in the vicinity. Apply insecticide or methylated spirit direct.

Take care
Avoid strong sun.

Ricinus communis coccineus
(Castor bean)
- Good light
- Temp: 13-18°C (55-65°F)
- Keep moist and fed

Oil extracted from this tropical African tree is used in medicine, and the leaves have an oily sheen. The coccineus form is superior, with a reddish hue to its leaves; it should be the one selected if there is a choice. In nature a height of 12m (40ft) is not out of the ordinary, but when roots are confined to pots it will be nearer 1.2-1.5m (4-5ft). Growth is fairly rapid, and plants may be stood outside during the summer.

A light position indoors will suit them best, and the room temperature should be cool rather than too hot. When potting on use a loam-based mixture and ensure that established plants are fed regularly: this will usually mean at every watering as new leaves develop.

In hot, dry conditions red spider mites will become a problem. Mites are generally on the undersides of the upper leaves and cause light brown discolouration.

Take care
Avoid hot, dry conditions.

Sansevieria 'Golden Hahnii'
(Golden bird's nest)
- **Good light**
- **Temp: 16-21°C (60-70°F)**
- **Avoid overwatering**

This one is rarely offered for sale today, because the plant is incredibly slow growing. There is also a plain green *S.* 'Hahnii', but it is not in the least attractive compared to the golden-coloured variety. Both make neat rosettes of overlapping leaves 10cm (4in) in length.

One of the best homes for them is a dry bottle garden; or they can be used in a dish garden. Like the more conventional sansevierias, both 'Hahnii' varieties abhor wet conditions, and will quickly succumb should the prevailing conditions offer a combination of wet and cold. Warm and dry will suit them very much better; in winter they will go for weeks on end without any water, and in some situations they could well go through the winter completely dry, as do most of the cacti and succulents. Feeding is not important, but a loam-based potting mix will be much better than one that is entirely peat.

Take care
Avoid cold and wetness.

Sansevieria trifasciata Laurentii
(Mother-in-law's tongue)
- **Good light**
- **Temp: 16-21°C (60-70°F)**
- **Keep dry**

This plant is almost indestructible. The leaves are about 60cm (2ft) long, thick and fleshy, holding a lot of moisture which the plant can draw on as needed; in view of this, it is important not to overwater, nor to give any more than the plant requires.

A good watering once each month in summer should suffice, with none at all during the winter months. This may seem harsh, but if plants are to be exposed to colder winter temperatures they will get through much better if the soil in the pot is dry rather than wet. Potting ought not to be done too frequently, and one can leave the plant until it actually breaks the pot in which it is growing – the swelling bases of leaves within the pot are quite capable of breaking clay as well as plastic pots. Loam-based soil is essential when potting on, and clay pots will help to maintain the balance of these top-heavy plants.

Take care
Avoid cold and wetness together. 134♦

147

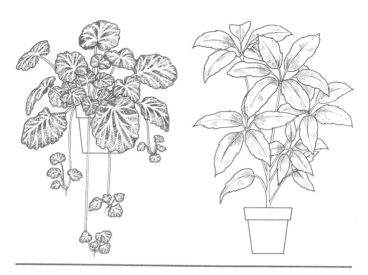

Saxifraga sarmentosa
(Mother of thousands)
- **Light shade**
- **Temp: 16-21°C (60-70°F)**
- **Keep moist and fed**

This is one of the simplest plants to propagate: you just detach the perfectly made plants when of reasonable size and press them into small pots filled with houseplant potting mixture. Grow the parent plant in a hanging basket with a curtain of tiny plants hanging from it and attached to threads of growth that may be 60cm (2ft) or more in length; the family of young plants will provide continual interest.

These plants are very easy to care for. Offer them reasonable light and warmth, with water and feed in moderation, bearing in mind that plants suspended from the ceiling will tend to dry out more rapidly than similar plants growing at a lower level in the same conditions. The amount of feed given will very often depend on the vigour of the plant, and during the winter months little or no feed is required.

Inspect these saxifrages regularly for pests: mealy bug, red spider or aphids might be present.

Take care
Suspend plants for best effect. 135♦

Schefflera digitata
(Umbrella plant)
- **Light shade**
- **Temp: 16-21°C (60-70°F)**
- **Keep moist and fed**

Even with roots confined to a pot, this majestic indoor tree may attain a height of 3m (10ft) or more. The glossy green palmate leaves radiate from the leaf petiole like the fingers of a hand. Unlike some houseplants, the schefflera does not produce more than one new shoot when the top is removed, so overgrown plants lose much of their charm when the growing top is severed. Also, as plants increase in height they tend to shed lower leaves.

New plants are raised from seed, normally sown in high temperatures in spring. When large enough, seedlings are put into small pots containing peaty mixture, later into larger pots of loam-based soil.

Indoors they respond to light, airy conditions, and the ideal temperature should be in the region of 18°C (65°F). They grow more vigorously in the warmer months, and need more water and regular feeding; in winter less water is needed and no feeding.

Take care
Avoid extremes of temperature.135♦

Schefflera venusta 'Starshine'

(Umbrella plant)
● Light shade
● Temp: 18-24°C (65-75°F)
● Keep watered and fed

This comparative newcomer has dark green glossy leaves, attached to the petiole like the fingers of a hand. Unlike the more common larger scheffleras, it has narrow, undulating leaves, with the result that the plant has a deal more elegance. It is also a much more compact plant, and will be better suited to the average home than the bolder schefflera types such as *S. digitata*. Avoid excessive watering and feed when active.

One problem is that the plant seems to attract mealy bugs, which will quickly spoil the appearance with their sticky, black honeydew if not dealt with. Honeydew is in fact a nice term for the excreta of the mealy bug, which drop onto the leaves below where the bugs are present, with the result that black fungus mould will form on the excreta. The latter can be wiped off with a sponge, and the mealy bugs can be removed with a swab of cotton wool soaked in methylated spirit.

Take care
Keep warm and draught-free. 136♦

Scindapsus aureus

(Devil's ivy)
● Light shade
● Temp: 16-21°C (60-70°F)
● Keep moist

S. aureus used to be one of those varieties that were difficult to propagate and to care for indoors. Yet we now have a plant with the same name that is one of the most reliable and one of the most colourful foliage plants available. It can only be that by constant re-selection a much tougher strain of the same plant has been evolved; there is now little difficulty in propagating it, and it seems to have an almost charmed life indoors.

Belonging to the Araceae family it needs a reasonable amount of moisture in the pot and, if possible, also in the surrounding atmosphere. The variegated leaves are green and gold, and for a variegated plant it has the truly amazing capacity of being able to retain its colouring in less well lit places. Most other variegated plants deteriorate or turn completely green if placed in locations offering insufficient light. The devil's ivy will also climb or trail as desired, and does well in hydroculture.

Take care
Avoid hot, dry conditions. 136♦

149

Scindapsus 'Marble Queen'
(Variegated devil's ivy)
- **Light shade**
- **Temp: 18-24°C (65-75°F)**
- **Keep moist and fed**

The white variegated devil's ivy will test the skill of the most accomplished grower. Most plants with a large area of white are a problem, and this is no exception.

A temperature over 18°C (65°F) is needed, particularly in winter. Also, it will be necessary to create a humid atmosphere around the plant. (This should not be confused with watering the plant to excess.) The simplest way is to provide a large saucer or tray filled with pebbles on which the plant can stand; the saucer can be partly filled with water, but the level should never be above the surface of the pebbles, as it is important that the plant pot should not stand in water. In a warm room such a saucer will continually give off moisture around the plant. Moist peat surrounding the pot in which the plant is growing is another way of providing moisture; and there are numerous types of troughs with capillary matting for placing plants on; these are useful at holiday time.

Take care
Keep moist and warm. 137♦

Sedum morganianum
(Burro's tail)
- **Light shade**
- **Temp: 13-18°C (55-65°F)**
- **Keep on dry side**

The burro's tail is a rather fascinating plant in that the fleshy grey leaves are closely grouped on slender hanging stems that give the strands of plants the appearance of a very meticulously plaited length of rope. One problem is that the small pads of growth are easily dislodged with handling. It should be grown in a hanging pot or basket.

However, suspending small pots overhead is fraught with danger as far as the plants are concerned, as it is extremely difficult to water them satisfactorily, and one also tends to forget them. When utilizing burro's tail as a hanging plant it is suggested that several small plants be put into the same container to give a bolder display and make their care easier. Mention is made above of hanging plants *above* one's head, but it is better to hang them at about head level so that they can be easily checked and tended. Use porous potting mixture, and keep plants on the dry side and in good light.

Take care
Handle carefully in transit. 137♦

Selaginella
(Creeping moss)
- **Shade**
- **Temp: 18-24°C (65-75°F)**
- **Keep moist**

These challenging plants, which will test the skills of the most accomplished grower of indoor plants, resemble miniature moss-like ferns, and are available in a number of varieties.

They require warm, moist conditions, and any drying out of the roots or the atmosphere results in shrivelling of foliage. When potting plants, use a mixture that will retain the maximum amount of moisture – a peat and fresh sphagnum moss composition is best. Foliage should be frequently misted over with tepid rain water, and the pot placed on wet gravel or plunged in damp peat. However, given all these requirements it will still be hard to keep these plants in an ordinary room. The moist, humid conditions they need are best created by using a sealed glass container, which will be free of draughts and has its own damp environment. Also ensure that plants are not exposed to direct sunlight, or close to radiators.

Take care
Ensure moist and warm conditions.

Senecio macro-glossus variegata
(Cape ivy)
- **Good light**
- **Temp: 13-21°C (55-70°F)**
- **Keep moist and fed**

In appearance these vigorous climbing plants strongly resemble the small-leaved ivies, and they must have some form of support for their rapid growth. During their growing season, provide moist conditions and regular feeding; less water is required in winter, and no feeding.

However well the plants may be cared for, in time the top growth extends and lower branches begin to shed their leaves. Replace older and less attractive specimens by starting afresh with a new batch of cuttings. Senecio will root like a weed during the summer if given warm and shaded conditions. Stem cuttings with two leaves attached should be prepared, and up to seven of these put into each small pot filled with peaty potting mixture.

This plant is prone to attack by aphids, which seem to find the tender succulent new growth particularly appetizing; inspect the tips for aphids, and treat with insecticide as soon as possible.

Take care
Inspect frequently for aphids.

Setcreasea purpurea
(Purple heart)
- **Good shade**
- **Temp: 10-16°C (50-60°F)**
- **Avoid wet conditions**

The humble tradescantia has many interesting relatives, including *S. purpurea*. Brilliant purple leaves are seen at their best when the plant is growing in good light with some direct sun, but very strong sun should be guarded against. They are impressive when grown in hanging pots or baskets: with all hanging plants one should endeavour to achieve a full effect, so lots of cuttings should go into each pot.

Cuttings of pieces of stem some 10cm (4in) long will not be hard to root in conventional houseplant potting mixture. Enclosing the cuttings in a small propagator, or even a sealed polythene bag, will reduce transpiration and speed up the rooting process. Several cuttings, up to five in each 7.5cm (3in) pot, will provide better plants than single pieces in the pot.

Like most of the tradescantia tribe, this one should be well watered and allowed to dry appreciably before watering again. Feed occasionally.

Take care
Replace old plants by cuttings. 138138♦

Sonerila margaritacea
(Frosted sonerila)
- **Light shade**
- **Temp: 18-24°C (65-75°F)**
- **Keep moist**

A neat and colourful plant, with prominent silver markings on the upper surface of leaves, and purple underneath. They are extremely difficult to manage if treated simply as a potted plant for the windowsill.

Low temperatures, draughts, full sun and overwatering all make life difficult for the tender sonerila. Sonerila demands even temperature and even amount of moisture above all. A glass case or bottle garden offers draught-free conditions that can also be maintained at an evenly moist level much more easily than can be done if plants are simply placed on a windowsill among cold draughts and fluctuating temperatures.

Use tepid rain water, not water drawn direct from the tap. Feed regularly with weak liquid fertilizer while plants are producing new leaves; when potting, they will do best in soilless mixture. Ensure that soilless mixtures do not become excessively wet or dry.

Take care
Avoid cold and wetness in winter.

Sparmannia africana
(Indoor lime)
- **Light shade**
- **Temp: 16-21°C (60-70°F)**
- **Keep moist and fed**

The sparmannia may produce a few flowers but is principally a foliage plant. The leaves are very large and fresh green in colour and are produced in quantity from woody stems. Small plants have straight stems, but they will begin to branch while reasonably young, and develop into attractive small trees.

The number of leaves and vigour of growth immediately suggest that this is a hungry plant that will require adequate and frequent feeding to retain its pleasing colour and maintain its vigor without loss of leaves. Older plants can be quite severely pruned at any time of year. Firm pieces of stem with a few leaves attached can be very easily rooted in peaty mixture in a temperature around 18°C (65°F). Use peat to start them off, but pot on into loam-based potting soil as soon as they have a reasonable amount of roots.

Mealy bug can be a problem, but is easily detected and can be wiped off with methylated spirit.

Take care
Remember to feed and pot on. 138♦

Stenotaphrum secundatum
(St Augustine's grass)
- **Light shade**
- **Temp: 10-16°C (50-60°F)**
- **Keep very moist and fed**

This amazingly invasive grass bounds away in all directions once it has established a foothold. It is not unattractive, with cream and green variegation, the cream being predominant. Its major drawback is that as the plant produces fresh growth, so the older growth shrivels and dies, leaving dry brown leaves hanging from the lower parts of the plant. However, if one has time to remove these as they appear, the plant can be kept looking attractive.

Tufts of grassy leaves with a thicker base are produced in profusion; any removed and pushed into pots of peaty soil root almost at once. When plants appear to be past their best, root fresh cuttings and dispose of the aged parent. This is best done in the autumn, so that one will have more manageable plants to care for over the winter.

These plants will grow anywhere if there is moisture and warmth, and are very welcome as something different in the way of hanging plants.

Take care
Renew older plants regularly. 139♦

153

Stromanthe amabilis
- Shade
- Temp: 18-24°C (65-75°F)
- Keep moist

This plant belongs to the same family as the calatheas and marantas. The oval-shaped leaves come to a point and are a bluish green in colour with bands of stronger colour running the length of the leaf. They overlap one another and are produced at soil level from a creeping rhizome. They reach a length of about 15-23cm (6-9in) and a width of 5cm (2in).

New plants are easily raised by dividing existing clumps into smaller sections and potting them up as individuals. The soil for this ought to be a good houseplant mixture containing a reasonable quantity of peat. Being squat plants they will also be better suited to shallow pans rather than full-depth pots. Shade is essential, as plants simply shrivel up when subjected to strong sunlight for any length of time. Soil should be kept moist, but it is absolutely necessary to ensure that it is moistness that is the aim and not total saturation.

Take care
Maintain warmth and humidity. 140♦

Tetrastigma voinierianum
(Chestnut vine)
- Light shade
- Temp: 16-21°C (60-70°F)
- Keep moist and well fed

Given moist conditions in a warm greenhouse and reasonable cultural care you can almost stand and watch this plant putting on new growth! The lobed leaves are a soft green in colour and are seen at their best when the plant has freedom to climb a supporting stake or framework. As new small leaves appear, so do the fascinating hair-covered tendrils which reach out in search of an object to cling to. This is probably the quickest growing of all indoor plants, and is ideal if one needs a climber to cover a wall trellis in the minimum time.

Being vigorous plants, they have to be kept on the move with frequent feeding, doubling the fertilizer dose that the manufacturer recommends. It also means that potting on cannot be neglected: large plants of chestnut vine in small pots will never do well. The potting mixture must be a loam-based one and the potting should be done with a degree of firmness.

Take care
Provide generous feeding. 141♦

Tillandsia usneoides
(Spanish moss)
- Light shade
- Temp: 16-21°C (60-70°F)
- Spray foliage frequently

One of the most fascinating plants of them all, in that it does not require any soil in which to grow. The plant has very slender stem-like leaves that form a tangled mass resembling a bundle of silvery-grey tangled wire. In their native Everglades of America these plants hang in dense masses from the branches of every tree.

A decorative few pieces on something like a small decorated bromeliad tree that is kept moist by frequent spraying can be a fascinating feature in the conservatory, where excess moisture will be easier to tolerate. Plants need only be hung over a branch. The clump will increase in size, and the strands in length. Ensure that the foliage is moistened regularly during the course of the day. Propagation means little more than teasing pieces away from the parent plant and hanging them up individually. Feeding is not necessary: other than water, the main need is for adequate warmth.

Take care
Keep foliage moist.

Tolmiea menziesii
(Pick-a-back plant)
- Light shade
- Temp: 7-18°C (45-65°F)
- Keep moist and fed

Interesting plants that develop into soft mounds of pale green foliage that are attractive at low level or suspended from the ceiling. Mature leaves develop perfect young plants that are carried on their backs. These can be detached when of reasonable size and potted up individually in peaty houseplant mixture. To succeed, plants should be kept in a light and airy place and be watered and fed with moderation. For mature plants use loam-based potting soil. Although they will tolerate very low temperatures and survive, they are better kept at around 16°C (60°F).

Hot and dry conditions increase the possibility of red spider mite infestation, which will in time considerably weaken plants. A sign of red spider presence will be a general hardening of the topmost leaves of the plant, which also become much paler. Check the undersides of leaves periodically with a magnifying glass; mites are very difficult to see otherwise.

Take care
Avoid hot and dry conditions. 141▸

155

Tradescantia blossfeldiana
- Good light
- Temp: 10-16°C (50-60°F)
- Keep on the dry side

This interesting and robust plant has pale green hairy foliage and stout stems, and is capable of withstanding rough treatment. There is also a variegated form, with pale cream to yellow colouring suffused through the paler background green, and a purplish underside to the leaves. Both produce the typical three-petaled tradescantia flowers, which are purple with white tips.

One frequently sees very weedy examples of these plants about, and the trouble seems to be that the initial plants had only a single, straggly cutting put in the pot. With plants that produce lots of growth, as tradescantias do, always put several cuttings in the pot when propagating; you will then have a full and handsome final plant.

With hanging baskets of plants that become ragged in appearance, remove the tops of half a dozen shoots and insert them where there are gaps. Tradescantia cuttings root almost anywhere.

Take care
Never overwater or overfeed.

Tradescantia purpurea
(Wandering Jew)
- Light shade
- Temp: 13-18°C (55-65°F)
- Keep moist and fed

This tradescantia has a brownish-red upper surface to its leaves and a purple underside, with fleshy, paler stems. Not so trailing as many of the tradescantias, it looks better growing in a shallow pan on the windowsill rather than in a hanging basket.

Cuttings with about three leaves can be taken during spring or summer and rooted in a houseplant potting mixture. Peat will not encourage them to root any better, and frequently results in the small plants being starved once they get under way. As with all the freer-growing tradescantias it will be best to put five to seven cuttings in the pot to ensure a fuller final plant. Excessive watering should be guarded against, but plants must remain moist during summer, and should also be regularly fed over this period. Towards the end of the summer more vigorous plants will have taken on a straggly, tired appearance, and it is then advisable to trim back any untidy growth.

Take care
Renew with cuttings periodically.

Tradescantia 'Quicksilver'
(Wandering Jew)
- **Good light**
- **Temp: 10-16°C (50-60°F)**
- **Keep on the dry side**

There are numerous varieties of *T. fluminensis,* but this one is bolder and much brighter than any of the others; all, however, require very similar treatment.

Good light is important if plants are to retain their silvered variegation, but protection from bright sun will be necessary. The soil should be free to drain and at no time become waterlogged. These plants respond well to regular applications of liquid fertilizer while they are in active growth. The view that when plants are fed they tend to lose their variegation is nonsense, as variegation depends on available light and whether or not the plants are allowed to become green. In poor light leaves tend to become green; and green shoots will in time take over, if not removed.

For baskets there are no better foliage plants, and small baskets or pots can be started by placing cuttings directly into the basket potting soil.

Take care
Remove green growth. 142♦

Vriesea mosaica
- **Light shade**
- **Temp: 16-21°C (60-70°F)**
- **Water into urn of leaves**

Some of the vrieseas are quite small and produce their flowering bracts at an early age, whereas others, such as *V. mosaica,* are grown principally for their decorative foliage. The colouring of *V. mosaica* is a dull reddish-brown, and there are interesting variations of colour through and across the leaf, as the name suggests.

This plant is quite rare and seldom offered for sale, but others of similar type are seen occasionally. Most have intricate patterns and colours in their recurving leaves, and grow to considerable size. They also have the typical bromeliad rosette of recurving leaves that makes a watertight urn into which water can be poured for the plant to live on. The urn should be kept topped up and the water replenished occasionally, but there is seldom need to water the soil in the pot – spillage from the urn is usually enough to keep the soil moist enough. All bromeliads do better in a mix of peat and coarse leaf mould.

Take care
Give very little water to the soil. 142♦

Yucca aloefolia
(Boundary plant)
- Good light
- Temp: 10-21°C (50-70°F)
- Keep on the dry side

The woody lengths of stem are imported from the tropics in very large quantities; they come in an assortment of sizes and are rooted at their destination, then potted and sold with their attractive aloe-like tufts of growth at the top of the stem.

Further benefits of this plant are that they are pleasing to the eye when grouped together, and little trouble to grow.

They do best in well-lit, coolish rooms if given the minimum of attention. The soil should be allowed to dry out quite appreciably between waterings and feed should be given once every 10 days during the summer months.

Purchased plants are normally in pots relevant to their height, so the pot is often quite large; as a result of this, the plant is growing in a container in which it can remain for two years or more. Plants should be potted on only when they have well filled their existing pots with roots. Use loam-based soil for this job when it is done.

Take care
Never overpot or overwater. 143♦

Zebrina pendula
(Silver inch plant)
- Good light
- Temp: 13-18°C (55-65°F)
- Keep moist and fed

This very common member of the tradescantia family has extraordinary colouring in its leaves, all of which have a plain purple reverse. It is one of the easiest plants to care for indoors, but the ease of care sometimes results in the plant being neglected.

Plants are very easily started from cuttings taken at any time other than winter. These should go into small pots filled with peaty soil, six or seven cuttings in each pot. Once established, put three or four pots of cuttings into a small hanging basket filled with a good houseplant potting soil, and keep the basket at a low level until the plants have obviously got under way; then the basket can be suspended at about head level. (If baskets are suspended immediately after planting, their care is often neglected.) Put plants in a light position out of direct sunlight, and water and feed them well while they are active; keep them dryish in winter, with no feeding.

Take care
Renew old plants every second year for an attractive display. 144♦

Index of common names

Dieffenbachia 'Tropic Snow'

PRINTED IN BELGIUM BY
proost
INTERNATIONAL BOOK PRODUCTION

Aucuba japonica variegata